PRAISE for *SYNCREATE*

Given the ever-increasing dominance of artificial intelligence and machine learning, cultivating massive creativity may be the most valuable skill for 21st century humans. But developing better right-brain functionality can be incredibly difficult without some kind of easy-to-follow process. Enter *Syncreate*, a simple but sophisticated twelve-chapter guide for individuals, teams, and communities who want to more successfully steer their creative journey.

—Hugh Forrest
South by Southwest (SXSW) | Chief Programming Officer
sxsw.com

Syncreate is a clear and nicely organized gem of a book, from multidisciplinary talented and experienced guides and role models. Its many features include exercises and anecdotes as well as specific strategies. You will become creatively empowered, individually and in community. Highly recommended.

—Ruth Richards, M.D., Ph.D.
Author of *Everyday Creativity and the Healthy Mind: Dynamic New Paths for Self and Society*, winner of a Silver Nautilus Award, and Coeditor of *Chaos and Nonlinear Psychology: Keys to Creativity in Mind and Life*

Syncreate is an essential creativity guide for individuals, teams, and organizations. Readers will travel through creative wilderness and emerge with new ways to work on projects and life-long dreams. Creative strategies and tools serve as a catalyst to unlock and expand creative collaboration.

—Terri Goslin-Jones, Ph.D.
Psychology/Creativity Studies Faculty
Saybrook University

In *Syncreate* the authors offer an accessible and forthright demystification of that most mysterious of human processes—creativity. This presentation deconstructs the creative process into small and remarkably doable steps that go far to slay the dragon of "overwhelm" that sabotages many creative endeavors. The contents of this book will benefit the creative efforts of individuals and groups with its organized, digestible approach and clearly stated suggestions and practical exercises.

—Karel James Bouse, Ph.D./Ph.D.
Author of *Neo-shamanism and Mental Health and Transgenerational Colonialism: Wounding, Overcoming and the Reconstruction of Collective and Personal Identity* and Director of the Institute of Esoteric Psychology

---

This is a phenomenal and well-written text for anyone interested in pursuing creativity in their life. The Syncreate process looks at everything important: the individual, team, and community process of creativity in a practical, yet poignant manner. It would be hard for anyone to finish this text and not play, plan and produce.

—Diana Rivera, M.A., P.C.C., Ph.D.
Creative Empowerment Coach and Facilitator
http://creativeempowermentcoaching.com

Truly beautiful piece of pedagogy . . . The anecdotes animate the instruction, the variety in spark suggestions enable any reader to find one that speaks to them. The enrichment information (theories, history, studies) grounds the instruction.

—Amy Katz
Writer, Former Educator

SYNCREATE

A Guide to Navigating the Creative Process for Individuals, Teams, and Communities

By Melinda Rothouse and Charlotte Gullick
with Dreux Carpenter

ISBN: 978-1-950186-33-4

Cover design and interior graphics by Dreux Carpenter
www.dscarpenterdesign.com

MANDORLA BOOKS
WWW.MANDORLABOOKS.COM

This book is dedicated to anyone who has ever had a creative dream and sought to bring it out into the world.

ACKNOWLEDGEMENTS

This book has been a long time coming. It represents years of work and wisdom gathered from our collaborative experiences with students and coaching clients, as well as the highs and lows of our own creative processes. Writing it has been a collective effort sparked by our synergy in working together over the years. Dreux Carpenter provided a great deal of insight and energy, helping to shape our ideas, giving feedback on our working drafts, creating the cover and designing the artful images interspersed throughout the book. John Best, a musician, software developer, and good friend, has also contributed greatly to the ideas explored here in terms of mapping the creative process.

We also want to thank all the courageous souls who have attended our creative gatherings, workshops, and events over the years, some of whom share their experiences in the quotes at the end of each chapter. Every time we gather with other creatives, we ourselves are enriched by the exchange. Our fellow Syncreators have taught us, again and again, the power of vulnerability, connection, and collaboration.

Additionally, we are grateful to our families, both near and far, the families we've chosen and those who have chosen us, who have supported us and believed in us—creativity is born through community.

Finally, we extend our deep gratitude to Jennifer Leigh Selig at Mandorla Books for believing in this work and championing us through the publication process.

TABLE OF CONTENTS

Introduction 1

Stage 1: Play - Creative Ideation, Skill Building, and Experimentation 13
Chapter 1: Creative Ideation - The Bird's Eye View 15
Chapter 2: Skill Building 25
Chapter 3: Experimentation 35

Stage 2: Plan - Mapping the Journey, Formalizing the Plan, Getting Lost and Finding Your Way 47
Chapter 4: Mapping the Journey 49
Chapter 5: Formalizing the Plan 59
Chapter 6: Getting Lost and Finding Your Way 71

Stage 3: Produce - Iteration, Collaboration, and Fruition 83
Chapter 7: Iteration 87
Chapter 8: The Power of Collaboration 99
Chapter 9: Fruition 107

Chapter 10: Teams and The Syncreate Process 117

Chapter 11: Communities and The Syncreate Process 127

Chapter 12: Syncreate Your Life 135

Bibliography and Recommended Resources 141

About the Authors 147

INTRODUCTION

Welcome to the Syncreate experience, your guide to navigating the creative process. Syncreate is both a noun and a verb; it's about the synergy of co-creation; it embodies the spirit of collaboration. We're excited that you're taking this journey with us. Based on our own experiences as artists, educators, and coaches, we felt inspired to write a book to help others understand and have better facility with the creative process. We've spent many years researching, discussing, and thinking through it, and we've developed a framework for moving through the stages from ideation to completion, from inspiration to finished product. We hope it will help get your artistic juices flowing. Think of it as an approach to creative project management that can be used by anyone from students to artists and individuals to organizational teams.

We define creativity very broadly, so when we use the word "creatives," we mean everyone, because all of us have the innate ability to be creative. Our brains have evolved to be adept at creative problem solving, innovation, and meaning-making, with an innate drive toward beauty and aesthetics. We also know from our own experiences, as well as those of our students, clients, and colleagues, that creativity can be difficult. We all experience blocks at some point or another, as well as self-doubt, loneliness, and a lack of inspiration and/or accountability. As many others have noted, the creative process can be fraught with challenges, detours, and zigzags. It's a nonlinear journey, and our aim is to help you find your way through this messy, circuitous route. We've been there and know the isolation and confusion that can come with following a process that doesn't have a clear map.

Turns out, getting lost in the process is actually a necessary aspect of creativity, and we encourage you to embrace this disorientation in two ways:

1. by helping you see that losing your way is essential
2. by showing you how to get back on track once you've wandered into the wilderness.

We've identified a method that allows you to get lost, get back on track, and cultivate the fruits of your journey with precision, clarity, and maybe even a little joy.

We believe that to be alive is to be creative. As John Daido Loori (the founder of Zen Mountain Monastery in Upstate New York and author of the book *The Zen of Creativity: Cultivating Your Artistic Life*) says, "Creativity is your birthright." We're here to unpack some of the myths about what it means to be creative, such as the myth of the tortured artist or the solitary genius going it alone. It can be empowering and also overwhelming to unlearn our stories associated with the process, and relate to creativity in a new way. If we embrace an expanded notion of the agility and facility of our imagination, we also have to be willing to work hard, get lost, and share our challenges. If we commit to the creative dreams we hold dear, it means we have to set small goals in order to achieve them—and we need others to help us meet those goals. If we accept that inspiration comes to those already in motion, we're more likely to start on the path, rather than wait for the spark of genius to get us going.

One caveat: we also want to acknowledge that producing a product is just one way of thinking about creativity. It's important to underscore the power of playing for playing's sake, without an outcome necessarily tied to this play. But, for those who do want to produce a specific result, we recommend you follow the steps outlined in the following chapters to arrive at the goal.

This book contains exercises, anecdotes, and specific strategies—all aimed to help you move with more confidence in the creative wilderness. It also offers new insights, connections, and a practical perspective you can share with other creatives in your life.

The Syncreate Team: Our Journey of Creativity

We'd like to share a little bit more about our team and how we came to work together. Creative exploration is at the heart of our connection. Charlotte and Melinda met while teaching at Austin Community College in Austin, Texas. We collaborated on developing a study abroad program combining religious studies (Melinda's field) and creative writing (Charlotte's field), and met regularly to explore how these disciplines might intersect. During the course of these meetings, we discovered a deep mutual interest in creativity, and a synergy that led us to explore how we could collaborate outside of academia.

Together we founded Syncreate to help to make visible the sometimes invisible process of creativity, both for ourselves and for others. Along the way, the Syncreate team has grown to include Dreux Carpenter, a graphic designer and creative writer who has accelerated our visual understanding of how to communicate our core ideas. Additionally, John Best, a musician and programmer, has made essential contributions to the development of our approach to the creative process. Our combined experiences in different artistic mediums, professional work, and academic training has shaped our insight into the creative process, which we have formalized into the Syncreate approach.

Our own collaboration has taught us the accelerating power of accountability partnership, which is at the core of our approach. We believe that in order for the journey of creativity to lead to fruition, we need others to help us break down the larger goals into incremental, actionable steps AND to help us make sure we are realistic in timelines and intentions. A weekly check-in with a like-minded soul can be the anchor we need to move forward with bringing our dreams into realities.

How Do We Syncreate?

Consider this book your ally as you move deeper into the adventure of creativity. Through our years of helping others complete their imaginative projects, we have found that the most common barriers to completion arrive with the following questions:

- Where do I start?
- What do I do next?
- How do I finish?

The Syncreate approach tackles each of these questions by breaking the creative process down into three main components: Play, Plan, and Produce. The following image (our

Syncreate logo) illustrates the interconnection between these three elements, and the recursive nature of creativity.

OVERVIEW OF THE CREATIVE PROCESS

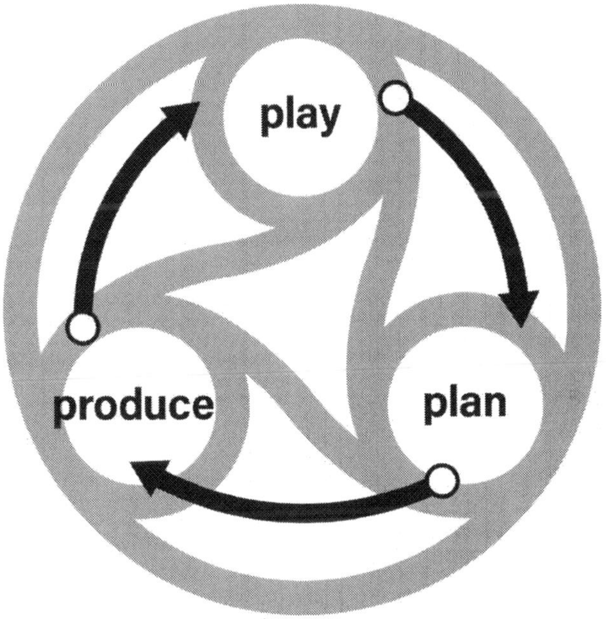

The Syncreate model draws inspiration from the major phases of creativity described by researchers over the years, beginning with Graham Wallas in 1926, who outlined four stages: preparation, incubation, illumination, and verification. Wallas' model might suggest that creativity is a linear process, whereas the Syncreate model, with its interconnected elements of Play, Plan, and Produce, affirms that the process is actually cyclical and iterative. Our method relates to other parallel approaches such as the lean startup model described by Eric Ries and the design thinking approach developed at IDEO. These emphasize prototyping, iteration, and refinement. Understanding these stages has empowered us and our clients to find more clarity and confidence in the creative journey.

Our approach offers a framework (rather than a formula) that accommodates a variety of creative styles, while incorporating incremental goals and accountability. To that end, the notion of Syncreate is based on two important ideas:

1) While the creative process is unique to each individual, there are consistent steps that, once recognized and articulated, can empower you to find your way forward.

2) We need to identify the smaller steps or tasks required to complete a project. With this micro-level precision, we are more likely to find traction with our creative work.

Convergent and Divergent Thinking

The stages of Play, Plan, and Produce also recognize two very different thinking modalities or brain functions required for the creative process. One is convergent or linear thinking, which includes logical, "left brain," rational thinking, planning, and other executive functioning tasks. The other is divergent or associative thinking, which emphasizes free-association, "right brain," stream-of-consciousness thinking, along with dreaming and envisioning. We discuss these two modes of thinking in more detail in Chapter 3. For an even deeper dive into convergent and divergent thinking, there are several good works on the topic included in the Recommended Resources at the end of this book.

It's important to understand that both types of thinking are absolutely necessary to bring a creative project to fruition, though many people tend to favor one over the other. Popular myths about so-called "right-brain" or "left-brain" people suggest that we excel in one area or the other, but not both. Think of the stereotype of the highly creative artist or musician with many great inspirations who spends so much time in the studio but never seems to bring anything to fruition. Or, on the other hand, the highly rational planner who is really good at making lists and creating beautiful spreadsheets but has difficulty thinking outside the box or generating new ideas.

We have come to understand that everyone uses both types of thinking and that we never truly separate one from the other. In fact, most of us intuitively know which kind of thinking is most useful in a given moment, and we instinctively move back and forth between these two types of thinking as needed. At Syncreate, we've learned that we can cultivate a greater awareness of and facility with convergence and divergence, which can give us greater creative freedom and joy.

How This Book is Organized

We've designed this book to guide readers, from total beginners to seasoned artists, through the creative process and to move from ideation to fruition on their projects. The creative journey can present challenges and roadblocks for most everyone, so we've created a roadmap to empower anyone with a creative idea.

Countering the myth of the solitary creative genius gifted with inspiration, we lay out a path that includes discipline, community, clear milestones, and concrete action plans as the necessary tools to finish what we start. Each chapter begins with a story or anecdote, followed by an in-depth exploration of one aspect of the creative process, and concludes with a series of creative sparks: prompts, activities, and exercises that help to provide an experiential learning component. Additionally, each chapter includes a personal account from someone who has worked with us using the Syncreate approach, describing how it has impacted their creative process.

The Artful Journey: Play, Plan, and Produce

In Chapters 1-3, we describe the first stage, Play. Here, we exercise our divergent thinking strengths to purposely engage the question of "What if?" This stage includes the original creative idea or inspiration, and this is where we get to:

- Daydream
- Experiment
- Enter the realm of possibilities
- Explore different ideas and techniques

In short, this is a time of potential, and in the spirit of play, a time to engage in the creative process with joy and curiosity.

In Chapters 4-6, we outline the second stage, Plan, where we develop an action plan for completing the project. This is the stage where we move from dreamer to do-er, including:

- Articulating the project's vision, mission, and values
- Mapping the journey
- Establishing goals, timelines, milestones, and accountability
- Working through creative blocks

Many of us do this naturally, in various ways, but few of us actually formalize this action plan when it comes to our creative work. Many of us lack formal accountability, in the form of commitment paired with follow-through. This is particularly true when we are responsible only to ourselves rather than to formal deadlines and other people, such as collaborators, employers, clients, etc. Creating and keeping to an action plan and deadlines can be especially difficult when we prioritize our creative work behind other important life necessities, such as our jobs, families, etc.

In Chapters 7-9 we review the third stage, Produce, in which we actually complete and refine the creative work with steps such as:

- Prototyping our designs
- Working through different drafts and iterations
- Getting feedback on our works in progress
- Engaging in collaboration and fruition/completion

This stage includes the countless hours spent at the computer writing the Great American Novel. Or composing, rehearsing, and recording that Grammy-winning album. Or in the art studio creating paintings or sculptures for the debut art opening. Collaboration and feedback are an important component of production. This phase culminates when we actually bring our ideas and creative work to fruition, bringing it out into the world for others to see, hear, and appreciate. Examples might include the dance premier or the unveiling of our latest photography exhibit.

We explore how Play, Plan, and Produce apply to teams and organizations in Chapter 10 with respect to idea generation, brainstorming, evaluation, and accountability. It's important to ground our understanding of these concepts in order to build real trust in the process. Innovation thrives when team members articulate and follow clear guidelines for their collaboration. Finally, Chapter 11 considers the power of community, detailing why creatives need to sustain and uphold one another. Creativity doesn't generally happen in a vacuum, but rather in response to real-world challenges, inspirations, and events. This is why community and collaboration are essential. We dive more explicitly into the process of collaboration and the importance of being in the company of like-minded folks, but for now, remember that building your creative community is just as important as your individual process.

We've laid out this method into three stages so that you can learn to toggle between the different moments of the creative process with a keener understanding of how you can intentionally find your waypoints during the journey. However, we also want to remind you again that this isn't a linear process—the stages we've described are different entry points into the cycle of creativity. We believe that there are many ways to enter the wilderness. Learning to toggle between them can enhance your creative practice.

The stages of Plan, Play, and Produce can help us to achieve our macro-level or big picture goals as well as our daily, micro-level activities. Whether we're talking about the project as a whole or the incremental steps we're taking to get there, we need to continually plan, play, and produce both on a small and on a large scale. This is an iterative (and re-iterative) process, all the way through.

It is also important to note that creativity is not only about problem solving but also about problem identification and definition. Indeed, creativity research shows that the better you can define the problem you are trying to solve in the first place, the better the solutions will be.

We consider the Syncreate perspective integral to our daily lives, both professionally and personally, and we hope it will enhance your own creativity, collaborations, and community connections. We're excited to share our insights with you.

STAGE 1

Play - Creative Ideation, Skill Building, and Experimentation

In Stage 1, we emphasize the importance of play as it relates to the creative process. In the journey from idea to fruition, we need to embrace not-knowing in order to build a sense of the map we'll need. We also need to bridge the gap between our desires and our abilities, and we can do this through a variety of specific methods. The key in this stage is to catch our ideas by honoring them with attention, caretaking, and joyful study and experimentation.

In Chapter 1, Creative Ideation, we discuss the beginnings of a project. This is the time where we pay attention to our dreams, obsessions, and fascinations and diligently track where our creative interests lie. This might mean keeping a photo or a dream journal, or otherwise tracking preoccupations and lingering questions about why the world works the way it does. We explore the concept of iteration and dive into the possibilities of *what if*. In other words, we say yes to our creative impulses by honoring them with our time and consideration.

In Chapter 2, Skill Building, we highlight the importance of developing expertise as a key aspect of closing the gap between our aspirations and our abilities. Practice, focused study, informal apprenticeship—these can all be forms of play that hone our skills. Most importantly, they become vital tools for harnessing the joy of process. We have come to see playfulness and joy as foundational approaches to develop skill in our given artistic medium.

In Chapter 3, Experimentation, we examine how experimentation generates new possibilities, as well as how it relates to convergent and divergent thinking. Also, adapting our approaches to a given project can empower us with the necessary agility to remain in sustained creativity. For example, imagine the aspiring potter who has not yet delighted in the visceral thrill of guiding clay into form, who has never touched a throwing wheel. While holding a fired piece of clay, rich with form, texture, and color, they experience a desire to create. Listening to this impulse, they humbly accept that play and practice are required to move into this new art form.

Play allows us to embrace curiosity and a sense of beginnings. This is the time to say yes to our ideas—there will be plenty of time to vet them later. If we begin to question them too soon, we can undercut some of our best possibilities. Learning to Syncreate means embracing play as an essential part of the creative process.

CHAPTER ONE

CREATIVE IDEATION—THE BIRD'S EYE VIEW

Melinda recently wrote a song called "Bottle of Rain," which is about seeing the beauty and magic in ordinary, everyday things. The guiding image of the song had been with her for over 20 years, when a friend brought her an extraordinary gift: rainwater he'd collected in a juice bottle during a summer storm while working in rural Kentucky. This turned out to be one of the most thoughtful gifts she'd ever received, and she has kept it ever since. Such a simple thing, and yet such a beautiful gesture. The first verse of the song is:

My heart is a fallow field
Just drinking in the dew
The still point, the fertile void
Just a broken arrow and a bottle of rain

We highlight this example because of the time period it covers: our creative impulses may live within us for years before we are ready to explore them, and embracing this gestation process can be a useful creative strategy.

This chapter honors the seeds of our creative work—inspiration and ideation—the birthplace of the complex and winding journey toward bringing our dreams and visions into the world.

Perhaps you've been daydreaming about a particular creative endeavor for years now, such as writing a memoir, or recording a record, and now you're finally ready to dive in. Or you have lots of ideas but you're struggling to decide where to focus. Maybe you're working on a grant proposal for a community art project, or you've been commissioned to create a particular work for a specific client. Whatever your creative challenge, there are specific strategies to help find your starting point and commit to a project.

It can be scary to pay attention to our ideas and interests—if we do, we are bound to change and grow, and that is not always easy. One may feel a paradoxical resistance to these creative desires. We've experienced this ourselves, yet we also know the joy of moving in the direction of an idea and living into the demands of bringing that creative spark fully into the world. We've known the challenge along with the satisfaction, and we've witnessed countless others who have as well. The final word? It's worth it.

The Whispers of the Creative Mind

Let's begin with the creative process itself. Where do novel ideas come from anyway? In order to understand how to engage with creative ideation, it is helpful to know something about how we discover creative possibilities, as well as the neuroscience of creativity. As we described in the Introduction, we believe that everyone is creative by virtue of being human. Our brains have evolved to be adaptive, problem-solving mechanisms. It's something we do naturally every day, perhaps without consciously realizing it.

One of the major ways that the brain generates new ideas is by finding links between seemingly unrelated things. For example, who was the first person to combine peanut butter and jelly into a sandwich? Initially, this probably seemed strange, but once it caught on, it became perfectly natural. Making these kinds of new connections is called associative or divergent thinking, and it is the lifeblood of creativity. The thing is, associative or divergent thinking requires us to let our minds roam freely, in a state of daydreaming or mind wandering—also known among creativity researchers as "defocused attention." This is why so many great insights actually happen when we're doing something physical such as walking or showering or sleeping and our minds are doing their own thing, unconstrained by linear thinking and focused attention.

We can learn to cultivate similar open mind states by allowing space for them and not trying to converge too soon. By recognizing that an open playing field is a major component of creativity, we can learn to separate the "being" from the "doing" by focusing on one part of the process at a time. If we try to cram both idea generation and fruition into the same space, we might actually be holding ourselves back.

If you're struggling to craft a creative idea or commit to a particular project, we recommend diligently paying attention to what captures your imagination and what interests you. What do you daydream and/or obsess about? What visions or images return again and again? Often there's a voice from somewhere deep inside whispering an idea, a poem, a set of lyrics, or a dream image that wants to manifest onto a canvas. Paying attention to the whispers of the creative mind requires us to quiet the often dominant, so-called left brain mode of planning and executive functioning and opening up to more imaginative, right-brain, nonlinear ways of thinking. Jill Bolte-Taylor, a former neuroscientist, has a powerful story about experiencing a stroke that impacted the left hemisphere of her brain, ushering her into a more right brain, creative, sensual, flow-like state. Her book and TED Talk *My Stroke of Insight* describe her experience.

Learning to pay deep attention to our creative impulses does not necessarily come easily, but we have to start somewhere. We recommend committing to regular creative time. For some people, the early mornings can be a good opportunity for this, before the rest of the world wakes up and the demands of daily life begin calling us. Melinda's daily morning practice includes meditation and journaling with a cup of coffee. This is her sacred space, and it is so important to her creative process, and to her general well-being. Similarly, Charlotte commits twenty minutes a day to her own creative tending. Sometimes this is the first thing she does when she wakes up and other days, it happens right before she goes to bed.

Dreamwork and the Creative Unconscious

Pay attention to your dreams. According to Jungian psychology, they are manifestations of the unconscious, the source of all creativity. Our dreams can carry important messages, images, and ideas that find their way into our creative work, if we remember and record them. A great way to practice remembering them is to keep a journal next to your bed, and to write down your dreams upon waking. Before going to sleep, it can also be helpful to set an intention, or a clear goal, to remember our dreams. Just like any other practice, the more we do it, the more natural it begins to feel.

Charlotte, during her first year at college, didn't know what her major should be or what path she needed to follow. During this time, she had a complicated dream involving a ritual of acceptance that involved passing a test of a spider "accepting" her. Upon waking, Charlotte wrote down these vivid and captivating images and years later worked them into an essay about accepting her role as a writer.

Embodiment and Creativity

One underappreciated but highly important element of the creative process centers on the body: we need to engage our embodied selves to access the full range of our ideas. This might run counter to what many of us believe about creativity being solely a mental activity rather than a somatic, full body enterprise. When possible, physical movement encourages ideas, connections, and insights, and it's essential to include opportunities for action such as walking, stretching, swimming, or biking as part of the way we engage with our creativity. Of course, this all depends on our options and abilities when it comes to our bodies. Find what works for you and your own embodied creativity.

Learning to trust our bodies is not necessarily easy, and yet, there is an emerging collection of research about the richness of our somatic awareness. Amanda Blake explores this rich terrain of somatic intelligence in her book *Your*

Body is Your Brain. Our mental engagement with the world is embedded in a web of knowing, that includes sensory input and automatic physiological responses. This allows us a variety of methods to connect with our inner and outer worlds, including memory and pre-verbal perceptions.

Movement is one way to tap into these other channels of information. In his book *The Courage to Create*, humanistic psychologist Rollo May describes this interconnection between our physical experience and everything around us, emphasizing that "the body is always a part of the world." Similarly, physical action can help us achieve a flow state in which everything falls away and we are completely engaged with whatever we are doing. Such flow states are often associated with creativity.

Most creatives, myself included, feed on a creative noise that clouds instead of expresses our vision. Melinda and Charlotte recognized the crux of my creativity and helped me discover my own creative path.

— Cheri Hartman
Writer & Artist

Playing "What If?"

Have you observed how children seem to come up with a never-ending supply of play scenarios featuring superheroes and monsters and fantastic worlds with endless possibilities? Part of creative ideation requires giving ourselves permission to return again and again to that place where anything is possible. This includes intentionally engaging our imaginations, so that we are unconstrained by the limits of "reality" as we know it. In order to bring anything new into being, we must first be able to dream and envision it in our mind's eye. Only then can we begin to manifest our creative ideas.

One way to prompt our visioning work is to ask "what if" questions. What if I remembered my dreams and wrote them down in a journal every morning? What if I wrote a song about my current heartbreak? What if I committed to completing my novel by the end of the year? What if there was a simple, but so far unexplored, technology to clean the world's oceans? What if I experimented with some new art supplies and different mediums? What if I approached every encounter with another human being as a learning opportunity?

These "what if" questions open up a space of possibilities, from which we can draw inspiration to form a vision for our creative work. Once we have a clear connection to our imaginal impulse, we can then take steps to realize it. But before we can move in any coherent direction, we must first have a clear sense of where we want to go and what we want to create.

The following section offers a series of creative prompts, or "sparks," to help fire up your creative imagination, cultivate associative thinking, and generate new ideas.

Creative Sparks for Ideation

Honor the Whispers of the Creative Mind: Keep a small notebook handy, or use a voice memo, notes app, or camera on your phone to record your creative ideas and inspirations as they occur throughout the day. Perhaps an image or phrase comes to mind that could work well for a song lyric or character study. To go deeper with this practice, take some time each day to allow your mind to wander and explore, noting where your thoughts go and recording them as they arise. This can be paired with meditation or mindfulness practice and journaling. This exercise has the potential to help us find our most compelling material.

Dream Journaling: Keep a journal next to your bed to record your dream images and insights upon waking for at least ten days. See how paying attention in this way might affect your creativity. Do you notice any recurring images or themes? According to the psychologist Carl Jung, dreams are messages from our unconscious, which is the wellspring of creativity. This strategic engagement with the unconscious can allow us to draw connections and associations in potent and meaningful ways.

Engage the Younger Self: Think back to when you were young and consider what you might have needed for your creative life. What stories/dances/images/music could have been beneficial for you at that age? As the writer Melissa Febos says, "Write the book your younger self needed." Generate a list of possibilities based on these reflections. This is another avenue to connect to the open playing field of divergent idea generation, and at the same time, invites a specific relationship with our younger self which can yield compelling insight into our current creative aspirations.

Photography as Inspiration: Using your camera phone, go outside (or stay inside), and take ten photos, including elements of the natural world and/or ordinary, human-created forms. Notice what draws your eye and what patterns emerge. What's already there that you can lean on for inspiration and connection? How can documenting your current circumstances reveal an inner impulse that you haven't tapped into before?

Formalizing the "What-Ifs": Create a specific list of "what ifs" for a project you are considering. Say you're working on a scene in a novel that feels dull and uninteresting for a reader. You might gift yourself ten possible "what ifs" to energize the material: what if I added another character to the scene? What if I set this scene in a different location? What if the weather changes dramatically so that my characters are forced to alter their plans? Such questions allow you to stretch what you think you know about the project. This playful exercise allows us to see our known world in new ways by actively cultivating divergent possibilities.

CHAPTER TWO

SKILL BUILDING

When she was in her early twenties, Charlotte had the opportunity to be trained as a river raft guide with an organization that took individuals with special needs on boating trips. Charlotte had spent her first two decades swimming in rivers, but those hours in the water did not teach her how to "read" a river like a raft guide. During the training her understanding of how to read rapids grew. Essentially, the task is learning to read the "tongue" of a river—it might seem easy at first, but how a boat enters the tongue determines the nature of the ride through the rapid. It feels like second-nature once learned, but there's a whole lot of "not knowing" and mistakes necessary for the skill to be fully embodied. After hours on the river, under the tutelage of an expert, Charlotte developed her ability to enter a rapid with the control necessary for a quality ride—which means balancing risk with enjoyment. This new skill allowed her to guide her clients through the rapids with more confidence and finesse. Riding a rapid is a lovely experience, full of visceral thrill and physical empowerment—and it's a lot more fun (and safer), if everyone stays in the boat.

This chapter focuses on how we develop the tools needed to realize our creative aspirations. We may think because we're familiar with a particular artistic medium, we should have some inherent competence in it. Ironically, having a little bit of knowledge might actually hold us back—we might expect ourselves to have expertise immediately. Rather, we need to learn to see the medium through a shifted, beginner's lens, and then commit ourselves to building our aptitude. Knowing that there are distinct stages of learning can empower us with patience and self-compassion; no one automatically acquires a new skill. Rather, persistence and determination fuel us as we move from novelty to mastery.

In order to do this, we must practice. It's a matter of repetition and trial; we have to build both our aptitude and our muscle memory so that we can move toward mastery. You may have heard how Malcom Gladwell describes this: it takes approximately 10,000 hours to develop proficiency in any given field. This can be a daunting task, so it's helpful to think of our entry into new creative mediums (or our development within an existing medium) as a kind of apprenticeship, where we humble ourselves, embrace our lack of know-how, and give ourselves the gift of time to learn by doing. Judith Barrington, in her book *Writing the Memoir* addresses this idea, noting that "a long apprenticeship is needed in literature as in any other field that requires the acquisition of skills." The bottom line is that it takes time, effort, and dedication to develop our craft.

Accepting that we are novices can be liberating: it allows us to move incrementally toward our desired level of ability, and seek out guidance from those who have more experience. We don't have to figure it all out on our own; teachers can help us learn where and how to focus our attention and efforts. Once we free ourselves from the burden of being instantly and independently good at something, we have the latitude to proceed, knowing that mistakes and first efforts are as essential to skill building as our passion and drive toward creating a final product.

Once we accept the reality that our ideas won't simply emerge from our imaginations whole and complete, we have the potent opportunity to embark on closing the gap between our ability and our aspirations. If you need some inspiration, watch Ira Glass's excerpted talk on "Storytelling," which asserts that we must produce a high volume of work in order to catch up to our creative desires. In the case of musicians, for example, it is through instruction, persistence, and skill building that their fingers become deft and nimble on their instruments.

We recommend several specific ways to help hone your skills.

Take a Class or Workshop

One surefire way to grow your ability is to study the craft you want to master. This might mean a one-day workshop, a 16-week community college class, or an online Master Class. Options include individual lessons, instruction in the technique of your particular medium, or a free guest lecture or artist talk. At its core, instruction allows us to recognize our newness to the game, to turn toward those who have studied the field, and glean what we can from their experience and insights. Think of it as a shortcut, one where we are learning from others who are more adept. This allows us to lean on the foundation of skill and knowledge that the instructor has developed over time.

Learning from others also gives us new ideas and inspirations that we might never have developed on our own. For example, after many years of writing songs alone in her room, using her own idiosyncratic method of converting her poetry into song lyrics, Melinda took a songwriting class which empowered her with new insights. She learned to write lyrics based more on imagery and freewriting than on thematic content and rhyme scheme. This freed her up to compose a song that was different from anything she had written before.

Practice as Play

In addition to studying and learning, we must also be willing to put the time into becoming more adept—we find it helpful to think of this aspect as playful practice. When working with clients on their creative projects, we like to focus on the *process* and *practice* as well as on the specific products. Thus, we encourage people to cultivate a regular (daily or weekly) practice. The more consistent time we devote to our art and our craft, the more fluid and productive we can become. It's the actual 10,000 hours that we must devote to our work to develop mastery.

Some days will be better than others; one morning we may wake up feeling energized and inspired, while the next we may feel tired, dull, and disengaged. This is totally normal. What distinguishes successful creatives is their willingness and ability to keep coming back to their work, even when feeling uninspired. It's about sitting down to write, or practicing your scales, or applying paint to the canvas, and making slow, steady progress over time. Sometimes it may feel like a chore, but the magic is in practicing no matter what. The more time and attention we put into our work, the more likely we are to derive some gems we can develop further.

We also encourage you to cultivate a sense of joy when building your skill. Since we must practice, why not challenge ourselves to find some small measure of enjoyment in it? Think of a toddler learning to walk. We weren't born knowing how to do this—we no doubt fell down a lot while learning. And hopefully, we were nurtured as we experimented with our bodies and gravity. Consider the small ways good caregivers support toddlers: the smiles and nods of those around us, and the cheers when we successfully took our first steps across the room. This engagement with patience, playfulness, and joy can shape our relationship to skill building.

Practice as play also grows our confidence. Once we have gained even the tiniest amount of prowess, we need to celebrate it. Confidence begets practice which in turn begets more confidence—it's a loop that we can hardwire into our understanding of the creative process. We can develop this type of confidence in our skills by exploring new genres as well as developing our primary medium. Diving into a tangentially related field allows us to maintain humility and joy. In any new field, we must start at the beginning. Embracing this aspect of the learning process can mitigate frustration.

It's important to note that plateaus are also part of this landscape—we must learn to measure the distance between where we started and where we are now, and always focus on the gains rather than the gaps. This kind of growth mindset, as described by psychologist Carol Dweck in her book *Mindset*, is extremely valuable to cultivate in any type of creative endeavor.

The idea of writing a full-blown memoir paralyzed me until Charlotte offered the following tip: Write down every scene, memory, joke, idea that comes to mind. Keep this list at the ready. Each day scan the list until a scene draws you in and write it. Every day.

This deliberate and sustained practice has somehow generated a momentum that continues to surprise me. Accompanying that energy has been an ever increasing ease at finding the right word, or crafting a lean, fat-free sentence. And even if those gems are rare, I'm trusting the process for the first time . . . and really jazzed about it!

— Amy Katz,
Writer, Former Educator

Study Work You Admire

If you are a writer, spend time reading published work, learn what makes it tick, and study how different authors effectively string sentences together, craft scenes, develop characters and use metaphors. If you are a musician, listen to different types of music, examine the elements of songwriting and composition, and observe how various musicians and composers layer sounds together to create a symphony or a pop song. Studying other works can often give us new ideas and strategies for how we might want to approach our own creative projects.

Woodshedding

Melinda first heard this term from a seasoned guitar player in New Orleans, who referred to his many hours of sequestered practice as "woodshedding." Come to find out this is actually a very common term in the musical world. According to musician and teacher Paul Klemperer:

> *The term woodshedding in jazz means more than just practicing. It is a recognition of the need to sequester oneself and dig into the hard mechanics of the music before you can come back and play with a group in public. There's something philosophical, almost religious, about the term. The musical treasures of jazz are not easily accessed. You have to dig deep into yourself, discipline yourself, become focused on the music and your instrument, before you can unlock the treasure chest.*
>
> *At the same time, woodshedding is a process of demystifying the music. The amazing solo, the intricate bebop melody, the complex rhythmic pattern, can be learned, if one is patient. It is a humbling but necessary chore, like chopping wood before you can start the fire. The term woodshedding, like the term "axe" (slang for your musical instrument), evokes images of rural, rootsy beginnings. It is a reminder, conscious or not, of the deep roots jazz has in the blues,*

gospel, and the merging of African and European musical traditions under slavery.

In this way, woodshedding is essential for completing a project—at times, it may not seem as if anything is actually changing, but because of our hours of work, an invisible idea becomes visible and knowable to the world. There are a variety of ways we can grow our skills—or in the jazz world, build our chops. This necessary aspect of the creative process grounds us as we develop the "moves" of the medium in which we want to express ourselves. If we return to the idea of toddlers learning to walk, it is in the hours of practice, of trial and error, that they develop the ability to confidently put one foot in front of the other. And in order to run or dance, we must first take those baby steps.

Creative Sparks for Skill Building

Learn Something New: Sign up for a class or workshop related to your creative medium or find a free online class or YouTube "how to" video. This can sharpen your craft, stimulate curiosity, and foster a sense of wonder. It's a concrete way to build your skills that provides additional structure and accountability to your learning process. Once you have completed the class, create a new piece of work that incorporates this new or enhanced knowledge.

Attend an Improv Class: Studying improvisation is a great way to engage with the "what if?" game, and it can build our confidence and flexibility. Improv is about saying yes to whatever occurs and being fully present in the moment, also known as mindfulness. It helps cultivate a positive perspective, which is essential to the creative life. It's also a wonderful way to connect with others, practice collaboration, and build community.

Study What You Love: Examine what makes a particular piece of creative work so effective. For example, pick a passage of one of your favorite writers and analyze their use of language. Or study the use of brush technique and texture by your favorite painters. Write a two-page journal entry, articulating to yourself why you admire this work. By identifying what we specifically appreciate about a given piece, we are closing the gap between our aspirations and our abilities.

Woodshed - Practice Your Craft: Commit at least 20 minutes per day or at least 90 minutes per week to growing your craft, and embrace this opportunity to move toward mastery through playful dedication. Regularly developing your skills, whether practicing your scales or refining your calligraphy technique, is the surest way toward mastery. It's the first step in building a strong foundation for your creative practice.

Engage in a Different Medium: Sometimes we become so invested in our favorite medium that we lose patience with ourselves. If you embark on a new creative activity outside of your primary interest, you purposely ground yourself in the novice position. Studying a new medium allows for the development of beginner's mind, rooted in humility, which is an important emotional foundation for creative work. This can also illustrate how far you've actually come, giving you a new perspective on your primary creative field, and providing fresh connections or associations for divergent thinking.

CHAPTER THREE

EXPERIMENTATION

Melinda began practicing mindfulness meditation initially for stress-relief and to deal with the pain and anxiety she felt after relocating to Austin from New Orleans after Hurricane Katrina, along with an extremely painful breakup of a long-term relationship. At first it was simply about becoming present and finding tools to deal with the inescapable reality of her situation. The practice helped her to work with the emotional intensity of her grief while breathing through her moment-to-moment experience.

But the path of meditation also opened up an opportunity for her to study contemplative arts and photography, an approach to creativity grounded in mindful attention to one's present-moment experience. As a classically trained singer who had spent years studying the art and craft of traditional concert music and opera, she found this contemplative approach to creativity incredibly liberating. It allowed her to engage and experiment with both her songwriting and other new art forms in a fresh and playful way. She dove into contemplative photography as a regular practice, eventually showing her work in art shows and festivals.

She also trained to become a teacher of contemplative arts and photography, leading workshops and retreats both in the US and internationally, sharing what she had learned about this mindfulness-based form of creative experimentation with both aspiring and established artists and photographers. Facilitating the exploration of such a novel approach to creativity and witnessing the joy and inspiration it has brought to others has been one of the most satisfying aspects of her career.

The theme of this chapter is experimentation, the third component of play. Once you have an idea, you begin to improvise, to shape and reshape it the way a potter works the clay on her potter's wheel. Once fired, the clay becomes solid, rigid and unchangeable, but during this stage it remains malleable; the possibilities are virtually endless.

In the quest for insight, we build on prior knowledge to find our way into what we don't yet know. In science, this is called hypothesis testing; a scientist formulates an idea about what might happen if . . . and then conducts an experiment to see if the hypothesis can either be proven or disproven. Whatever the result, we learn something in the process. New creative work comes about in a similar way.

We know from neuroscience and the psychology of creativity that our brains use metaphor to extrapolate from what we already know into the realm of the unknown. For example, a musician might study the classics to learn the fundamentals of her craft. Informed by what has come before, she then creates her own compositions, gradually developing her own unique style. Or, using the process of divergent or associative thinking, she might draw from both her musical knowledge and her knowledge of another domain, such as visual art or mathematics, to synthesize seemingly disparate ideas into something new. Indeed, this is how Einstein began to formulate his theory of relativity, drawing on an intuitive understanding of space and time that he developed through his musical training.

Moving Outside the Comfort Zone

We have to risk what we think we know in order to create new combinations and associations. In this stage, we have to carefully listen to our imaginations and say yes to them, even when we don't know, yet, how to bring those ideas into being. Playing allows us to explore and to test our limits. Experimentation gives us the freedom to make mistakes and move from the limiting, binary mental construct of success vs. failure to the realm of growth. Embracing possibilities, we learn more about our medium, our given project, our ways of thinking, and our resistance or stuck points.

Experimentation also requires letting go of what we think we already know. Buddhist teacher Suzuki Roshi speaks to this process in his book *Zen Mind, Beginner's Mind*, observing: "In the beginner's mind, there are many possibilities, but in the expert's there are few." But, what does this actually mean? This statement seems to turn the conventional wisdom of expertise and specialization, so prized in our culture, firmly on its head.

Suzuki recognizes that in the journey to expertise, something is lost along the way. When a scientist or scholar first begins to learn about their field of study, the possibilities are endless, but as they continue to deepen their learning, they must pick a very narrow, specific area of specialization. However, as expertise and certainty in one area increase, other possibilities and avenues of exploration must be cast aside.

Suzuki reveals how meditation and mindfulness practices can bring us back to the sense of openness we felt at the beginning of the journey, where anything and everything was possible. This is the realm of creativity. Like a traveler just setting off on an adventure, we enter a space where everything awaits and nothing is yet certain. This is the foundational, humble position of possibilities, and we can return to it again and again, in every moment, and particularly at the beginning of a creative project.

In the writing process, we must embrace three archetypes: the child, the architect, and the judge. It can be helpful to embrace the child's mindset because this is the place of creative risk and imaginative opportunity. If we start to judge or organize our ideas too soon (converge), we might actually undercut the depth and quality of our conceptual frameworks. Children often color outside the lines, and they ask the most basic, but profound questions, like "What if there was no air?" (beginner's mind). Melinda's younger sister once asked that question, to which their father crisply replied, "Well, we'd all be dead" (expert's mind). Children have the freedom and flexibility to riff on the "what ifs" of the world without censure. If we can engage this divergent mindset, we open ourselves to new combinations and approaches.

Charlotte is both a fiction and nonfiction writer, but in both genres, she draws from personal experience. When she writes fiction, she thinks back on the potent moments of her life, and asks herself, "What if?" What if the mother left that night instead of staying? What if the sheriff did arrive in the middle of the night? Of course, much of creativity is asking the what if, but in Charlotte's case, she stays specific and grounded to what she knows, and this kind of "what if" is something she calls "the shadow plot." In the case of fiction writing, consider these questions: What if there were an alternative universe where the events went differently? How can you look to the past and see a different trajectory? And in that seeing, can you forge a story that feels, true, engaging, and concrete?

This approach can be so fruitful because it makes the familiar new. The novelist John Barth in his book, *The Tidewater Tales*, explores the relationship between two characters, and at the center of the story is a retelling of *The Odyssey* in terms of an embryo. Barth fuses the ancient story with a more contemporary setting: a married couple, their sailing adventures, and a possible pregnancy. This offers readers fresh insight into both new and old worlds.

At the beginning of a project, we need to be willing to diverge—if we converge too soon, we're limiting our capabilities. If we invite the architect or the judge in too soon, we might short circuit the creative process. Later on, we will need the architect to help us evaluate the structure and the organization, and the judge to carefully consider each decision of the project.

If we can learn to tease out these different aspects of ourselves, knowing when to call upon each of them, we can gain more facility and agency with the creative process. To be clear, understanding and accepting these distinct kinds of thinking takes practice and a cultivation of mindfulness. We develop agility with these elements, once we recognize their roles and when it is best to use them.

Many times we want to rush toward a finished product, inspired either by deadlines or simply the drive toward completion, rather than taking the time for improvisation and play. Again, think of jazz, where there is no written score or orchestration for a piece of music: the players spontaneously create a sonic tapestry, riffing off each other to create something new in the moment, based on their unique skills and training. Engaging with experimentation results from the necessary discipline and skill building discussed in the previous chapter.

Similarly, in theatrical improvisation, players gather to create a performance without a pre-set script. The task is to be fully present, working with whatever is there, to create a scene and an evolving narrative. One of the basic rules of improv is "yes, and," in which each player takes what is offered and adds to it rather than rejecting it, generating a space of ever-opening possibilities. This is the mindset we adopt when we experiment and play in our own creativity.

With a light, playful air, Charlotte and Melinda created an inviting community with space for all kinds of creatives to explore creativity, whether someone was a visual artist, performer, or writer. The experiential exercises were presented in an engaging way and I deepened my already familiar creative process with new awareness and appreciation.

Syncreate supports the challenging landscape of being an artist. It offers a system of accountability to check in regularly and celebrate our accomplishments.

—Kerry Kittrell
Artist, Creatrix
kerrykitrellart.com

A Deeper Dive into Divergent and Convergent Thinking

As we discussed in the Introduction, the creative process requires both divergent and convergent thinking, illustrated on the following page. Divergent thinking is associative; it's the more spontaneous of the two. It's about drawing connections between two seemingly unrelated things and generating new ideas. By contrast, convergent thinking brings ideas together into something more focused and coherent. We utilize both types of thinking in the creative process, toggling between the two. We must be intentional about when to brainstorm and generate new ideas, versus when to focus and pull these new ideas together. Understanding the difference between convergent and divergent thinking empowers us with more options in a given phase of the project. Consciously shifting between them when needed grants us more mastery in the creative journey.

For example, on the days when we feel less focused—rather than feeling disconnected and overwhelmed—we can say, "For now I'm going to just hang out with the ideas and see what emerges." We can see what connections unfold by means of associative thinking. Knowing there is more than one way to approach our material can unlock how we think about it. In fact, we have been able to write this book because of the "toggling" approach. We have learned to tune into our enthusiasm and energy levels and ask ourselves: What kind of thinking will best serve the project in this moment? Is today one where we focus our attention on editing, evaluating, and overall coherence, or could we work better by focusing on generating new material? In other words, we all have choices about when to employ convergent and divergent thinking, and which is best for the project at a given time.

DIVERGENT & CONVERGENT THINKING

DIVERGENT THINKING

c = challenge
i = idea

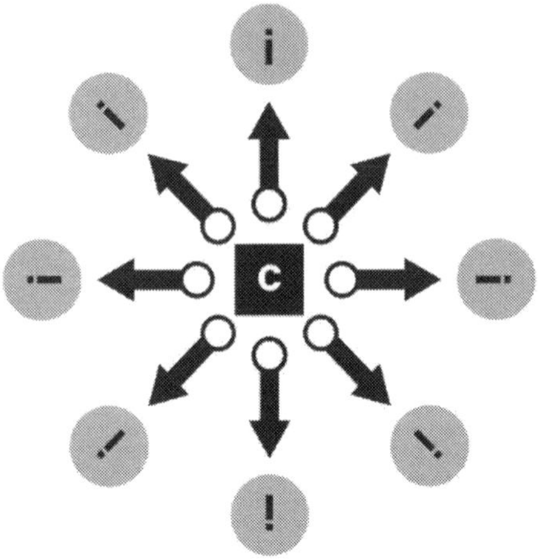

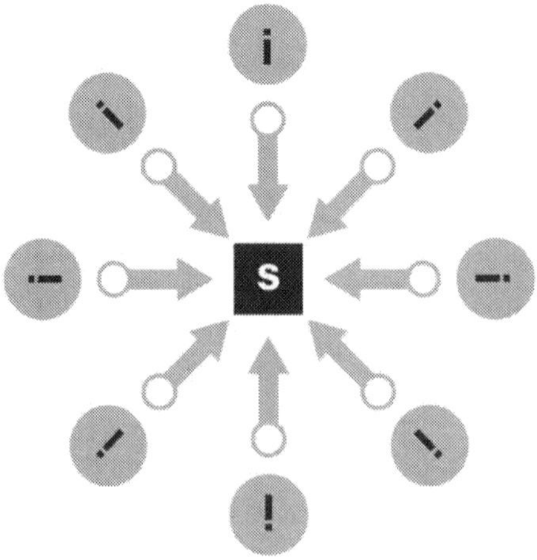

CONVERGENT THINKING

i = idea
s = solution

Indeed, returning to divergent thinking near the end of a project can also help us take it to the next level. There may be moments where we think, "Everything has already been done. I have nothing new to offer." It may **feel** like we have nothing original to add. However, if we remember that divergent thinking allows us to arrive at new combinations, associations, and connections, we may discover that we do have something fresh to say. To illustrate, one creative challenge we gave ourselves was to think of a familiar storyline and update it. We landed on a modern re-telling of the classic Dickens novel *Great Expectations* that explores racial equity in the U.S., surprising ourselves with the energy and insights we generated. Perhaps one definition of creativity is the willingness to see the known world through new lenses.

In the experimentation phase, we need permission to noodle around with the project and try different approaches, such as convergent and divergent thinking. This requires committing to the project so that we develop a sense of "muscle memory," or familiarity with, it so we can routinely re-enter it with more ease and grace. Like skill building, experimentation takes dedication and a willingness to not be perfect at our chosen art form. This commitment allows us a flexibility of method and vision.

In Chapters 1-3, we have described Play, the initial phase of the creative process, which includes creative ideation, skill building, and experimentation. This stage may yield a preliminary draft or a nascent version of a project. It is not yet complete or finalized, but it has begun to take on a distinct shape because we have explored and diverged, because we have tried out different ideas, rejecting some and accepting others. We have accepted that to grow our abilities, we need time to play and practice, in order to close the gap between our aspirations and our abilities.

Creative Sparks for Experimentation

Mix it Up: Create a mixed-media piece by actively incorporating an element from another creative field into your primary project (this requires both convergent and divergent thinking), and notice the associations and connections that arise. For example, if you are a photographer, print some of your photos and then cut them up to create a collage, thus using your existing creations to make something entirely new. If you are a writer, try incorporating drawings or images into your work, perhaps to create an illustrated book or graphic novel.

Explore Possibilities: Write a short story with five possible endings (divergent thinking) to decide which is the best one (convergent thinking). In this exercise, you are being asked to purposefully toggle between the two kinds of thinking so that you can become more adept at moving between them. In the process you might find a wildly apt metaphor that invites greater clarity and insight. This is a type of hypothesis testing in that you are asking yourself to prove whether or not a given idea is as viable on the page as it is in your imagination.

Embrace Constraint: Write a mini-memoir (1,000 words or less) and choose two different ways of telling the story: one might focus on the narrator and the other might evoke compassion about someone else in the piece. The limited word choice makes us focus (converge) and the varying perspectives allow us to play with possibilities (diverge). For some inspiration, read the article "Using Fiction within Nonfiction to Navigate Difficult Emotional Terrain" by Judith Padow. This form of experimentation actively engages constraint as a method for exploring ideas and "testing" them against one another.

Work with Clay: Take a pottery class without any expectation; focus on process and possibility. Working with clay allows one to experience the tangible process of creation. Also, you get to work with the unanticipated elements of trial and error. For example: How did that glaze turn out once fired? Did the piece break inside the kiln? How does a single point of pressure from a pinky finger alter the shape of things? Working in this physical way also helps you move out of the thinking mind to be present with experimentation.

Begin a Meditation Practice: Try visiting a meditation center for instruction in how to meditate, or try one of the many great apps that offer a wide array of guided meditations. Building a meditation practice can train our minds both to focus and open to possibilities, with the side benefit of highlighting our thought patterns and worries. Meditation teaches us to be present, rather than dwelling in the past (what's already happened) or anticipating the future (what we think might happen). In fact, the present moment is the space where new ideas actually arise.

STAGE 2

Plan - Mapping the Journey, Formalizing the Plan, and Getting Lost and Finding Your Way

Now that we've explored the divergent, exploratory realm of Play (Stage 1), it's time to begin thinking about goals, timelines, and action, which is the focus of Stage 2, Plan. Many of our coaching clients approach us when they realize it's time to put their creative work on the front burner, but they're unsure where to begin or how to go about it. The planning stage involves developing an action plan (goals, tasks, milestones, a timeline, interim deadlines, and accountability).

Many of us do this naturally in some form, but few of us actually formalize this action plan to emphasize accountability and completion. This is especially true when we answer only to ourselves rather than to formal deadlines and other people, such as collaborators, employers, clients, etc. Identifying and keeping to an action plan can be particularly difficult when we prioritize other important life necessities, such as our jobs and families, before our creative work. This stage also includes creative blocks and frustrations that inevitably arise in connection with the creative process, which we've characterized as "getting lost and finding your way."

In Chapter 4, Mapping the Journey, we share strategies for translating our ideas into a tangible action plan. This includes creating statements for our mission, vision, and values for the project, which serve as touchstones throughout the journey. Chapter 5, Formalizing the Plan, discusses how we can put that plan into action and stick to our goals, including working with accountability partners. Chapter 6, Getting Lost and Finding Your Way, helps us navigate the inevitably messy terrain of getting lost in the creative process and then finding our way again.

CHAPTER FOUR

MAPPING THE JOURNEY

Charlotte had an idea—she wanted to write a modern Western with a female protagonist—and she could see the climax: her main character Zane on a horse, gun at her side, on task to rescue her sister. The vision was exciting and clear, but in order to anchor this project, she needed a map to guide the writing. She had to define what progress would look like so she wouldn't get lost. She found a way to hold herself accountable to the incremental tasks that led to the larger goals, providing herself with lots of small victories (such as word count or number of hours per week writing). These micro goals built upon one another until she finished the novel's first draft; then she revised again and again, using the mapped micro goals to find her way.

This is an approach many people use, and it's available to us all. This is where we move from dreamer to do-er, from someone who fantasizes about a creative project to someone who completes it. At this point on the journey, many people stall out—they've experimented a little, they've built some basic skills—but now they must turn the idea into reality. This chapter guides us through the initial steps necessary for completion.

In the process of mapping the journey, we strategically move from divergent into convergent thinking, and we refer to it as creative project management. For some artists, this term can feel a little too formal, a little too close to the language of the business world, but we contend that this is an essential step in moving from ideation to fruition. Creative project management allows us to know ourselves: if we can document when and where we work best, if we can pinpoint our best practices, we can break down future barriers to our creative aspirations. Along with skill building and experimenting, we need to develop a set of incremental goals so that we remain committed to our project. This is the point where we identify where we are in the creative journey and map out where we want to go.

Having a plan allows us to commit to the incremental milestones required to make progress toward our final goal. Of course, we encourage play and a sense of openness at all times, but there are moments when we must move into a convergent mindset, otherwise our ideas remain in the ether. Without some kind of plan, we are far more likely to remain stuck and frustrated. Some of us internalize this feeling as a lack of talent rather than an issue of mindset. Indeed, having a project plan is how people who produce a lot of creative work get it done. They break the task down into manageable chunks, hold themselves accountable to those chunks via micro goals, and stay committed to them.

In this way, we must quantify our creativity—not because it's a commodity, but because it allows us to build traction and momentum.

Pulling Down the Sky

So, you've been listening to the inner voice, deeply considering the images and themes that your thoughts return to, but what happens next? Now you hone your understanding and then practice turning an idea into a viable project, one that has the potential for concrete fruition. There's a movement in chi gong called "Pulling Down the Sky" where you bring your arms out wide and up overhead, then down in front of the body's midline, bringing fresh energy from the sky down into your body. Moving from ideation to manifestation is a bit like this in the sense that you're pulling something from the ether of your imagination into tangible reality. This chapter and the next discuss how to create concrete, actionable steps that build momentum for your projects and move them into physical reality.

We know from our teaching and coaching work that people often stall out at this point in the creative journey. They might still be operating under the myth that inspiration will get the job done. We're sorry to tell you, from firsthand experience as creative practitioners and from coaching others, that an amazing idea isn't enough in itself. Just think of how many inspirations you or your friends have had over the years for a new invention, a business venture, or a handy gadget that never actually found its way to the light of day. The thing that separates a great idea from a viable finished product is follow through, and that requires planning. The good news is that there are steps you can take to move the vision into reality.

We actually find this quite liberating—rather than operating under the burden of elusive inspiration, we each have the power to create a roadmap that will guide us through the creative wilderness. It's been a crucial awakening for us and for our clients: if we equip ourselves with a plan, a map, and a timeline divided into incremental or micro goals, we can complete the journey. A quote attributed to the Buddha states, "If we are facing in the right direction, all we have to do is keep walking."

By mapping the journey, we can funnel the seeds of possibility (divergent thinking) into a specific set of micro goals and milestones (convergent thinking.) For example, in Melinda's Ph.D. program, she was given a handbook that laid out exactly how the dissertation should be organized, including what content should go into each chapter, how the text should be formatted, down to the font size and precise use of headings. While it didn't provide guidance on the actual writing process, this handbook provided a very helpful roadmap for creating and organizing the dissertation. Another example of mapping the journey is painting by numbers. This approach to art offers a formula that is extremely prescriptive, as it not only contains the pre-drawn image but also tells you exactly which color should go in each area, which doesn't leave much room for creativity but can be helpful for beginners. Both illustrate the importance of breaking a larger project down into a set of smaller tasks and achievable goals.

Mission, Vision, and Values

When embarking on a new project, an essential task is to create a vision or mission statement for yourself. This could be one word or phrase; it could be a collage of images; it could be a hummed line of melody. Whatever you choose, taking the time to clarify the feeling or image can become a lightning rod for helping us understand the purpose and scope of the project. Additionally, establishing a mission and vision can help motivate us later if we lose touch with what originally set us in motion.

Businesses and organizations (if they are wise) spend significant time developing their mission, vision, and values statements. These statements help both employees and clients understand what the organization aims to accomplish, what it stands for, and its guiding principles. When you go to a museum or gallery show, you will often find an artistic statement in which the creator shares their mission and vision for the artwork displayed, what inspired it, and so on. Similarly, many coaches encourage their clients to create a life purpose statement and spend time thinking about their top values, which can then serve as a touchstone, particularly when challenges arise. Such statements can also help guide decision-making when faced with particular choices or opportunities, creatively speaking. For example, if you are a musician and someone asks to use one of your songs in their commercial or their independent film, what would you say? Would it depend on the type of product in question, or the message of the film? Having a clear sense of your mission, vision, and values could help guide your decision making. For example, when evaluating new opportunities, consider if they are in line with your values, with who you are, and with what you're about artistically.

Melinda's work with creativity and productivity is incredible. She has helped me find the confidence and build the skills to jump into several new projects I had been wanting to tackle for years. She offers kindness and a dynamic flexibility that makes creativity a pleasure, while maintaining a high bar of excellence - a balance that is both rare and valuable in highly creative people. I'm confident that any creative professional could benefit from reading this book and understanding this approach to creative work.

—Daniel Whiteside
Mindfulness Teacher and Conscious Creator
danieljwhiteside.com

Creating an Action Plan

Once you have established your mission, vision, and values, it's time to begin crafting an action plan. Rather than a rigid set of rules, it is meant to be a flexible set of waypoints that will morph, grow, and evolve. Without these essential tools and guideposts along the way, we may be more likely to succumb to the pitfalls of creative blocks and losing momentum. Having an action plan can help prevent depression, hopelessness, and self-loathing, which in turn can undermine our sense of worth and possibility.

Perhaps you feel a bit of resistance about formulating a plan—that's not what we see in the movie montage where the novice gains mastery in a single week. We're asking you to acknowledge that resistance and create a plan anyway. There's no downside here: weaving in action steps can only increase the likelihood of a successful outcome. In this way, embracing the accountability factor can be an essential aspect of becoming more empowered. We've learned that the best way to make progress toward big goals is to start with incremental steps. To quote the Taoist sage, Lao-tzu, "The journey of a thousand miles begins with a single step."

Motivation and Building Momentum

If you accept the premise that fruition requires more than inspiration and genius, you've probably had some experience with the difference between intrinsic (internal) vs. extrinsic (external) motivation. Creativity researchers such as Teresa Amabile have found that a blend of both intrinsic and extrinsic motivation are important for the creative process. We can be intrinsically motivated by that initial spark of inspiration and by specific goals, but also extrinsically motivated by deadlines and having to be accountable to someone besides ourselves. Many of us struggle to create based solely on the internal sense of reward we feel. Therefore, we also need some element of external motivation in order to make incremental progress toward finishing the project.

This is why many people take classes, hire a coach, or find an accountability partner—we need someone or something outside of our own inner landscape to help us meet our micro goals. Additionally, we can slowly move ourselves toward intrinsic satisfaction by working with external deadlines as the mechanism to get us started; once we build our confidence and our muscle memory, we may eventually become less reliant on external forces to help us move forward. We begin to live into the feeling of small progress. Regular contact with the expression of our idea makes it so we can create momentum. We contend that connection begets connection, meaning that a consistent pattern of working toward small goals empowers us with confidence and purpose.

In short, deadlines matter—they help us produce and make imperfect progress. Rather than waiting for the right inspiration or the perfect conditions to create a painting, a chapter, or a song, deadlines force us to produce. Constraints can even make us more creative. A deadline can get us in motion where we might otherwise stall: knowing we are going to meet our writing coach in two days can make it so we prioritize our work and push through the ambiguity and awkwardness of not knowing how to proceed.

It's also important to create micro goals that are realistic. We have to be careful not to self-sabotage by asking the impossible of ourselves. As we know from the approach to goal setting known as SMART (Specific, Measurable, Achievable, Relevant, and Time-Bound), if we have a clear understanding of what is reasonable, we are much more likely to make the progress we want. It's easy to fall into the trap of "true talent," such as telling ourselves "If I were really creative or inspired, I'd be able to write 10,000 words a week." This false notion of what is realistic can undermine our ability to make progress. Setting such unrealistic goals can prevent us from truly committing to our creative aspirations. On the other hand, once we accept that slow but steady progress is key, we are empowered to move toward fruition. In the next chapter, we discuss in more detail the elements of a good action plan.

Creative Sparks for Mapping the Journey

Create an Outline or Mind Map (a graphic or visual representation): What is the guiding vision for the content and scope of this project? This could take the form of a traditional written outline or a word cloud or visual diagram—anything that allows you to get your ideas down on paper, or on a whiteboard, on your computer, or using a mind-mapping app. Having a visual layout allows us to conceptualize the work, rather than trying to hold it all in our minds. This physical act is another step in pulling our ideas from the ether into the real world.

Create a Linear or Visual Timeline: This timeline can be an essential tool in making sure you have a concrete map to guide the process, including a final completion date and deadlines for specific milestones. Again, simply creating the timeline can make the project feel more tangible. It also allows you to en-vision exactly how it will come into being, including the specific action steps needed for completion.

Journal About Your Resistance: If you are finding it difficult to create an outline or mind map, do some freewriting on why you might be feeling reluctant to articulate a plan. What's at stake for you here, particularly if you are not generally inclined toward planning, list-making, and/or project management? You might be surprised about what comes up. Are there any clues or insights that reveal a way forward?

Craft a Creative Mission or Artist's Statement: Creating a mission statement and explicitly articulating your vision and values can be another great way to gain clarity on the "why" of your project. These statements contain both your inspiration and what you hope to achieve. Write them out and post them prominently in your studio or workspace.

Consider Your Audience: We've found it can be quite helpful to step back from a project every now and then and ask ourselves—how might others experience this? You can sharpen your understanding of the possible take-aways for others by doing this writing prompt: What do you want people to come away with, to think, feel, or do after experiencing your creative work? Identifying the intentions of our work can help us translate our ideas to others, and at the same time, allow us to map the direction of our material.

CHAPTER FIVE

FORMALIZING THE PLAN

One of the myths of creativity is that we do it all on our own. There are a few rare individuals for whom this may be true, but for the majority of us, we need other people. One of the most profound elements of the journey is having people who help us define our micro goals and commit to them. Again and again, we have seen how accountability helps people move into their aspirations.

To quote one of Charlotte's former students, "There were several moments of revelation for me during the semester. First was the ongoing discussion from the other students and the continuous insight and feedback from the instructor. This information was priceless and opened my views on the genre and writing. I will be honest here (why would I be anything else?) the peer reviews were super scary, at first, but they proved to be incredibly valuable after they were complete." Being part of a community helps us be accountable to the goals we long to accomplish but often cannot do on our own.

If we can humble ourselves to connect with other like-minded folks on the creative path, we are much more likely to get where we—and they—want to go.

Okay—you've turned the page, which means you're open to the idea that having a plan is necessary. Congratulations! Based on our experiences teaching students and coaching clients through their creative projects, we appreciate the power of planning, even if our plans change along the way. As we discussed in the previous chapter, it's important to identify tangible goals and timelines for the creative process in order to visualize where we are heading. Then we can break the larger goals down into smaller, more tangible tasks that we can undertake on a daily, weekly, and monthly basis.

Just a quick reminder before we dive into the specifics of having a plan—this is a loose game plan, one that will change. That's part of WHY it works, because it's flexible enough to accommodate adjustments but firm enough to help us make progress.

We're not here to tell you what your plan should look like, specifically. We understand that each person's creative process is unique; some of us are more linear and deadline-driven by nature, more inclined to making lists and outlines and knocking them out. Others are motivated and inspired by other kinds of rewards, such as the satisfaction of completion, a daily inspirational quote, or a walk in nature before entering into a creative work period. This is why we do not advocate for specific tools or strategies, such as outlining vs. mind-mapping, or particular organizational apps. One of the challenges of the creative process is to identify the methods that work best for you and to put them to work in support of your goals.

Having talked a lot in Part 1 about divergent or associative thinking and its importance to creative ideation, it's time to focus on convergent thinking, which is the more linear, goal-driven part of the creative process. In Chapter 4 we introduced the concept of creative project management; now we will explore what it means and how to engage with it. Again, though we don't advocate for one particular tool of creative project management over another, we affirm the importance of planning and accountability. This could be as simple as laying out your project goals, milestones, and action items on a whiteboard, or keeping a log book or spreadsheet to track progress. Nowadays, there are many apps designed for individuals and teams to manage their creative projects. They can be extremely helpful, especially for teams collaborating on complex projects. However, you don't need a fancy app to manage your creative projects effectively, especially if you're working individually. But whatever tool you do select, you need to make sure it works for you and that you stay accountable to it.

Accountability is key, and this is what makes coaching so effective; it establishes a partnership that helps us prioritize and achieve our creative goals more effectively than many of us can do on our own. Another benefit of accountability is that we learn how to coach ourselves into meeting our own goals. So let's turn our attention now to the actual process of creative project management, which starts with developing an action plan.

Creative minds are cherished for their ability to effortlessly explode with an array of ideas. Sometimes, the smallest prompt can open their creative floodgates. However, knowing how to contain that explosion, take a collection of those ideas, and structure them into an executable set of tasks can seem equally as impossible. In my roles as both a professional musician and a Chief Technology Officer, I find myself using the tools of the Syncreate method daily to address both directions of this divergent-convergent circle. Syncreate helps me establish the correct environment I need to create that explosion of ideas, and also helps me organize those ideas, and the tasks needed to realize them, into an actionable order of precedence. For creatives who struggle getting a project completed, establishing accountability through rewarding micro goals and milestones gives a subtle and gentle push to keep moving forward.

—John F. Best
CTO, Thrive360

Essentials of a Good Action Plan:

- **The Vision**: This can take the form of an image, phrase, photo or musical idea that reminds you of what inspired you to begin this project.

- **Milestones and Micro Goals**: These are the tasks and incremental steps you need to complete in order to make progress.

- **Accountability Partner(s)**: These are the people you regularly check in with to help you stay on track by meeting milestones and micro goals.

Vision: The Creative Spark or Inspiration

Often our inspiration begins with a flash of insight or an idea that spurs us to start a creative project. This creative spark holds great power to keep us connected to our inspiration as we progress through the messy and often grueling work of bringing our ideas into being. Manifesting is hard, but good work! It can be useful to create tangible reminders, such as:

- Quotes or mantras that we post in our workspace
- A vision board to remind us of our larger purpose
- A musical playlist to keep us energized

It's easy to get distracted by the demands of daily life and to lose our inspiration somewhere along the way in a thicket of self-doubt. So, anything that can help keep us connected to our purpose is a great help.

Milestones and Micro Goals

How do we begin to identify our milestones and micro goals? The first step is breaking your project into smaller chunks. Here is an example of how micro goals can become waypoints along the larger creative journey: If you want to write a novel, you can organize your thinking to focus on the smaller, incremental stages that lead to the completion of a book-length project. When working on your first full draft, you can divide the work into smaller milestones. For instance, if you sense that your book might have 20 chapters, your action plan might look something like this:

- Drafting ½ of a chapter per week = 40 weeks to complete a full draft of the book.

Or, alternatively:

- Most novels have between 60,000-90,000 words. Say you want to write a 75,000-word novel. You want to have a full first draft six months from now, and you have two days a week to write. So, that's 52 writing sessions. Divide 75,000 by 52 and that equals 1,442. So, each writing session should produce roughly 1,442 words.

We know that creating a timeline isn't necessarily a sexy way to engage with creativity, but it is the way to get things done so that we can get to the final product. This is just one example to illustrate the power and importance of creating micro goals. We can use similar incremental steps or tasks to empower our progress in any artistic medium. The next image provides a visual representation of how to create a timeline that breaks the project down into incremental tasks and goals.

PROJECT TIMELINE

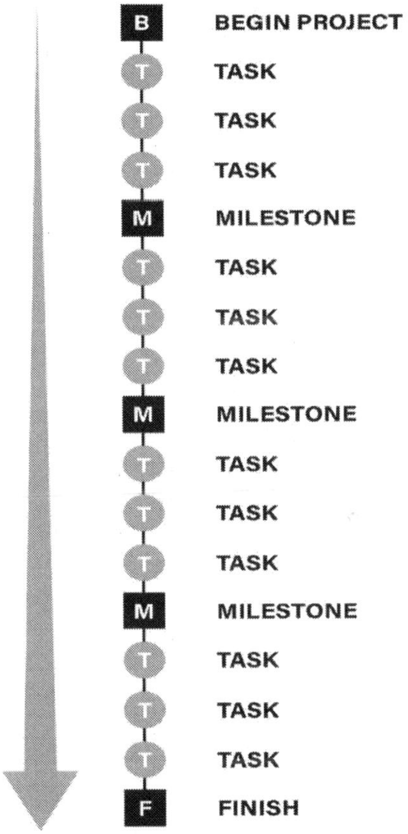

Accountability Partners

As we have stated before, having an external deadline can be an essential framework for bringing our ideas into the world. Accountability partners affirm our micro goals and hold us to our commitments. They don't have to be involved directly—rather, they are the people that help you externalize your action steps. It might be a coach, friend, or colleague with whom you check in via text or email. This interaction can be brief; it could take less than one minute. But for many of us, reporting to someone else might be the determining factor in whether or not we make our desired progress. Indeed, a 2013 University of Scranton study found that only 8% of people stick with their New Year's Resolutions. The reason why? No accountability.

Additionally, accountability partners help prevent self-sabotage in at least two ways:

- Externalizing our goals
- Assessing their feasibility

Once we externalize our internal creative desires, we have already begun to take the necessary steps toward completion, and such partners can also help us assess whether these incremental goals are realistic. For example, we might have a tendency to ask too much of ourselves, laying out impossible objectives, and this can undercut our momentum. This is often the case with exercise, where we might say to ourselves, "I will exercise every day this week," and then when we miss the second day, the whole week is shot because we haven't met the unrealistic goal. That said, we do want to differentiate between audacious versus unrealistic goals. The first type asks us to stretch outside of our comfort zones and envision new possibilities, while the other hobbles us even before we start. Identifying and articulating realistic but ambitious goals allows us to make tangible progress, especially if we engage the support of accountability partners.

It's also important to choose such partners with care. We might be tempted to ask a family member, but sometimes, this can become an emotionally challenging proposition. For example, a parent or partner is not necessarily the ideal person to check in with you about a project because the preexisting relationship dynamics could cloud the way we communicate and respond.

Having a "clean" emotional connection, one focused on the project, can be a wiser choice. It's essential to find someone firm in their resolve to help us reach our small milestones but who can also offer compassion and patience when the plans shift or we struggle in meeting our deadlines. If we are avoiding our incremental steps, we need this person to reveal our blind spots. A good accountability partner can help us articulate our resistance and assist us in working through it. It might be that the milestone goals simply need a little adjustment. It's not that we need to abandon the entire project; it could be that some finessing of the plan is necessary.

We can also serve as accountability partners for others. It's a wonderful part of being an artist: knowing we are not alone in the journey and that we are helping others along their paths. Engaging with others in this type of dialogue around our micro goals helps us progress with a sense of community and connection, thereby increasing the likelihood that we all stick to our action plans. In this way, creativity and accountability fuel each other in a positive reinforcement loop.

Faith Tenders

A faith tender is similar to an accountability partner, though less focused on concrete goals and action items, and more focused on supporting and encouraging us through the challenges of the creative process. In this case, a supportive partner or family member can be a great cheerleader for us. This could also be a work colleague or trusted friend who occasionally checks in with us about our project. Our faith tenders remind us that we can do it, that we have the talent and the drive to carry on when we lose our way. They also help us keep the flame of inspiration lit, as we traverse the darker corridors of the creative journey. Sometimes, just hearing, "I believe in you" can make all the difference.

Planning for Success

Ultimately, a realistic, well defined plan paves the way for success. We need the feeling of progress and traction in order to sustain ourselves over the long haul. By clearly and thoughtfully delineating our micro goals and tasks, we forge a path to fruition. At the same time, accountability partners and faith tenders anchor us to our commitments. Once we accept these realities, we can truly pull down the sky.

Creative Sparks for Formalizing the Plan

Create a Milestone Map: Using the project goals and milestones identified in the previous chapter's exercise, break down each milestone into a series of micro goals and deadlines so that you have a working action plan for the project. This step commits you more fully to the pathway, in tangible and concrete terms, so you can move in the direction of your creative goals.

Develop an Accountability Partnership: Seek out an accountability partner and start talking or meeting with that person regularly to discuss your project and action plan. This is a rich opportunity to connect with someone who can help support and champion your project, encourage you to pick up the threads when you get lost or lose steam, give you honest feedback, or help adjust the action plan if needed. You might find another creative working in the same medium, or in a different one, and offer to be that person's accountability partner as well, with an appointed time for weekly progress check-ins.

Focus the Work: Post an image, phrase/mantra, photo, mind-map or vision board somewhere in your creative workspace that affirms your initial spark. Sometimes when we get into the trenches of our project, we can lose touch with the initial joy or impulse that excited us in the first place. By reconnecting with the guiding idea or principle, we can toggle between the larger vision and the details of our work.

Find a Faith Tender: Since the creative process can be a time of self-doubt and getting lost, identifying one or two people who help you hold the vision for your project is essential.

These are the people who can remind you of how awesome you are when you lose your inspiration. Be judicious in choosing your faith tenders; these are people who look at the world—and your project—with optimism and hope for what is possible.

Plan a Small Reward or Celebration: Honoring our incremental steps and acknowledging what we have accomplished along the way is important for our ongoing motivation. Depending on your budget or sensibilities, plan a hike, a massage, a dinner out, or perhaps even a day of doing absolutely nothing as a reward for completing a milestone.

CHAPTER SIX

GETTING LOST AND FINDING YOUR WAY

Almost inevitably, at some point in our creative journey we are bound to falter, lose the thread of our inspiration, or wonder why we even began in the first place. If we can find a way to understand and accept this part of the process, perhaps even to welcome it, we can recognize the gifts it brings. Melinda experienced this dark night of the soul as she was writing her dissertation. She had conducted her research, analyzed and compiled her data, and was drafting findings when she lost momentum and fell into an abyss of apathy and despair. She lost sight of the project's parameters, got mired in the details, and wondered why she had ever decided to pursue a Ph.D. At that moment, she had become disoriented, uncertain that she would ever be able to pull everything together . . . and the clock was ticking.

Fortunately, she had some inkling that this was actually part of the process. A former client had recommended Robert Romanyshyn's book, The Wounded Researcher, *which suggests that getting lost is actually essential to a good project. The book traces the Greek myth of Orpheus and Euridice in relation to research, scholarship, and composition, showing how the archetypal journey of the Orphic descent, dismemberment, and reintegration cycle relate to the creative process. Romanyshyn illuminates how letting go of your preconceived, ego-based ideas for the work is in fact necessary for its full fruition. Believe it or not, this process of getting lost and descending into confusion and despair is often an indication that we're on the right path. The alchemy of the creative process will challenge and change us, as it should.*

As this story illustrates, creation can sometimes be an ordeal, and even a rite of passage. What happens when we lose our way, lose our minds, lose our inspiration, lose our will to go on? And what of the pain of birthing and completion? Only surrender will suffice. Many have described the stages of the creative process as though it is linear and straightforward. But creativity is messy: it invites chaos, doubt, dread, and moments of groundlessness.

The inner critic and feelings of self-doubt are universal; they are steadfast features of the creative landscape. Everyone has them, and learning to acknowledge how fear creeps into our journey is essential to maintain momentum and faith. Your inner critic may already be trying to undercut your project by whispering that real artists don't work with micro goals or accountability partners, but we're here to testify that real artists do indeed empower themselves with these potent tools.

This chapter helps us find a way forward when we get stuck in the creative process, feel blocked, or when our inspiration fizzles. When this happens, it can be disheartening and disconcerting. What began with a wave of energy and inspiration has shifted; we feel lost and confused, despairing of ever finding our way to completion. We may question ourselves, our abilities, and our motivations:

- "What was I thinking when I started?"
- "Who am I to take on this project?"
- "I've completely lost the thread and I don't even know what I'm doing anymore."

Over the years of navigating our own creative journeys and those of our students, clients, and peers, we've come to value this moment of crisis and doubt. Rather than being an anomaly or signaling that something is wrong, it's actually a natural, and perhaps even vital, part of the creative process. By embracing this, we can develop a healthier, more finessed understanding of ourselves and the necessary challenges we must accept in order to bring our ideas into fruition.

Creativity is an alchemical process in that we will be challenged, disoriented, and transformed. It begins with the "call to adventure," as Joseph Campbell terms the start of the hero's journey; it's what powers our creative impulses. Psychologist Linda Schierse Leonard explores this call to adventure in her book *The Call to Create.* Often when receiving the call, it's tempting to resist it, which is also a natural part of the process. As we embark, we encounter many challenges as well as helpers and guides to assist us. Then inevitably, at some point we also reach the abyss, the proverbial dark night of the soul, in which we question everything, seeing no way forward. Paradoxically, this stage often marks the gateway to transformation, or the creative breakthrough, allowing us to bring our work into the world.

Understanding that getting lost and losing motivation are important hallmarks of the journey allows us to carry on through the darkness. If we understand this beforehand, we will be less likely to abandon a project. Knowing that deep challenges are part of the landscape, we can allow for setbacks, doubt, and humility.

We are teaching ourselves persistence as we unmask the mystery of the creative process. We can let go of the myth that inspiration alone is enough, and there we sit, in the midst of our uncertainty: Does this project have meaning? Am I the person to complete it? Take a deep breath: this is exactly where we should be.

Jazz pianist Bill Evans put it this way: "Knowing that the problem is large," the creator must "take it a step at a time and . . . enjoy the learning procedure." We contend that once we develop a game plan, we provide ourselves with the necessary map to embrace a journey into the wilderness. It's helpful to distinguish between two aspects of getting lost: incubation vs. avoidance. The map we have already created may help us decide where we are in the process.

Incubation and Avoidance: Recognizing the Difference

A common pitfall of the creative process, particularly when we are feeling stuck, is avoidance. If we find ourselves avoiding our work, it could be for a variety of reasons. Perhaps the excellence we strive for isn't yet within our reach—this is known to many as perfectionism. We can become paralyzed by the risk of vulnerability and looking less-than-stellar. Our inner critic is there to protect us from looking foolish, but it can also limit the risks we take.

Remember, many good creative works begin with tentative or awkward initial attempts. If we determine that we are indeed avoiding our work, then compassion, patience, and trust can help us move forward. Beating ourselves up for not engaging in the creative process doesn't usually generate motivation. Similarly, overthinking rarely moves us out of our blockages; sometimes we simply need to move into action in order to face our avoidance. If we can lean into our sense of curiosity and wonder about where the project might go, we're less likely to avoid working on it. Taking action of any kind, such as journaling about the project or noodling around with some musical notes, can foster the momentum needed to return to the work.

Sometimes when we get stuck, we actually need to step away from the project for a while to let it marinate. This is known as incubation (rather than avoidance) and it's actually an important part of the creative process. Many writers and researchers have discussed the importance of strategically stepping away for creative insight. In his 1926 book, *The Art of Thought,* Graham Wallace describes four stages of the creative process: preparation, incubation, illumination, verification. Often overlooked and undervalued, the incubation stage is in fact vitally important in getting lost and finding your way. Perhaps paradoxically, taking a break from actively creating or thinking through a challenge actually helps to evoke insight. The incubation stage is the yin to the yang of actively planning and creating. It's more like daydreaming than problem solving, when we gain the necessary perspective we need in order to move forward.

Perhaps the insight or solution comes in a dream, when we are in the shower, while we are taking a walk . . . It's important to acknowledge and allow space for the incubation stage. Part of creative mastery is trusting that when we get lost we will at some point find our way again. Sometimes we need to step away, to embrace uncertainty and not knowing. From a depth-psychological perspective, can we allow ourselves to delve into the depths of the unconscious and let it work its magic? Can we surrender to the alchemical process of creation?

When in doubt, slow down. Be still, descend. The ability to hang out with uncertainty is a type of intentional incubation, or what Melinda refers to as "the still point." This is the energy of the black hole at the center of each galaxy, powering the spinning of celestial bodies and solar systems. It's the clear, still space at the eye of the hurricane; it's that quiet place where true insight can emerge if we get stuck.

The Taoists refer to this type of skillful retreat as *wu-wei*, or actionless/effortless action. Perhaps counterintuitively, this quiet space can offer us new insight into our current project. We might not actually be stuck; rather we might need to listen to what the project needs rather than imposing what we think we know about it. Psychologist Dan Siegel calls this dipping down into non-action or not-knowing as touching into the "plane of possibility": it's the space where anything is possible.

When we take action, it's a step in manifesting our ideas. At the same time, stepping into action also limits our choices because we are moving in a single direction rather than in all the possible directions. This is where a meditation or mindfulness practice can be very helpful: choosing to sit and be present allows us to tap into the full range of possibilities before taking any action rather than being swept into chaotic worry.

While this aspect of the creative journey is not always fun or pleasant, it can be an affirmation that we're on the right track. The process of creating art should change us somehow—it can transmute emotion, offer insights, and shift old patterns. Like the archetype of the hero or the notion of pilgrimage, in which the traveler is changed by the path, transformation cannot happen without a crisis of faith. Letting go of what we thought we knew about the project or ourselves allows a new perspective to arrive.

Embracing the uncertainty of the still point can be easier if we have front-loaded our creative journey for success. If we have formalized the plan and devised the infrastructure to anchor us, we're more likely to make the necessary leaps into the unknown and/or invite in the quiet of incubation. Instead of feeling desperate or disconnected from our project, we can accept the ambiguity of our current position. In other words, it's easier to dive into not knowing if we have a scaffolding to lean on. The importance of micro goals and accountability partners cannot be emphasized enough here: these elements seed our fruition.

I can honestly credit Syncreate as the turning point in my creative journey. It has been nearly eight years since I last doubted whether or not I was an artist. Charlotte and Melinda created a space for me early in my career that helped me concretely claim my artistry, and I have been flowing in the evolution of that empowerment ever since. Forever grateful to the magic of these women.

—Amelia Isabel Torres
Artist & Space Holder for the Human Experience
ameliaisabel.com
Instagram: @ameliasabelt

Returning to Play, Recovering Inspiration

In addition to asking for support and challenge from our accountability partners, we can also return to play. If we allow ourselves to consider the material with a liberated and possibly even a mischievous sensibility, we can defuse any negative emotional charge. When we become too serious, too focused on the outcomes, we rob ourselves of the sense of possibility that drives inspiration.

But wait, you're thinking—isn't play just another form of procrastination? It can be, but it doesn't have to be. Returning to play is a potent tool, especially when the project starts to feel like a burden. Rearranging our emotional outlook might help us find our way and our momentum again. Also, if we have the micro goals and accountability partners in place, we cannot stray too far afield from the desire we initially demonstrated in committing to the plan. Perhaps it's a two-day hiatus from the project to "fill the well," as Julia Cameron, author of *The Artist's Way*, describes it.

Another method for finding your way is to return to the mission or vision that initially sparked the journey. Think back: what was it about this project that initially excited and motivated you? Could ten minutes of journaling help you access those feelings again? Could coffee or a phone call with an accountability partner or a faith tender remind you of why this work felt important and engaging?

We also recommend studying work you admire. Let's take an example from poetry: There's an elegance to the distilled written word that can ground us. The way a poem falls down the page can inspire a dance gesture; the rhythm of the lines can help us with the song we're writing, or the images can guide our painting. And for writers, the right combination of noun and verb can sometimes unlock the phrasing needed to complete a chapter.

Some authors keep a collection of their favorite poetry by other authors handy for inspiration and sustenance as they begin their own drafting process. Poets have done the work of finding the most precise language and imagery to express a thought, feeling, or experience, and remembering our inspirations can be a determining factor in whether or not we continue. In addition to the poets, we can review the masters of our given medium to help guide or jumpstart our process. Museums and art books, dance performances and albums; all of these can become mentor moments where we brush up against and plunge into the work of people we admire.

Another essential aspect of finding our way through the creative wilderness concerns recognizing the difference between solitude and isolation. Of course, it's necessary to spend time by ourselves when we are deep in the process of creative experimentation and alchemy. On the other hand, we need to recognize when it's time to reach out and connect or collaborate with others. The connection of accountability partners isn't just about whether or not we're meeting the micro goals; it's also about the human relationship that grounds our ability to leap into the unknown.

We also understand how priorities can shift; perhaps the two hours a day you've allotted for your creative work have evaporated due to a family member's illness. This can produce anxiety and a sense of conflicting obligations, and we encourage compassion for yourself and the situation. Remember, you are still living your life and supporting someone else in a dynamic and grounded manner. You are still moving through the world as a creative being. Small moments of self-connection can help sustain you during these periods of shifted priority: perhaps you journal for five minutes upon waking and/or right before bed. Find opportunities to stay connected so that you don't feel a sense of detachment and alienation from your creative project. These micro connections can be powerful.

On the other hand, perhaps you have yet to achieve the creative skills or the maturity to complete a creative project. If you hit a wall, and you discern that it isn't about avoidance, you can give yourself permission to step back for a little while. This doesn't necessarily mean you are abandoning your work; instead, it might indicate you need some perspective or new life experience before returning to the project. Try not to feel bad or irresponsible in such moments. Rather, embrace the possibility that time away is exactly what you need. Returning to play and mentorship may develop the necessary insight to complete the project.

Creative Sparks for Getting Lost and Finding Your Way

Study the Hero's Journey: You are the protagonist in your own creative story. Study the hero's journey (described by the anthropologist Joseph Campbell in the documentary and book, *The Power of Myth*, with Bill Moyers) to see how yours compares, both with its highlights and challenges. Knowing that you are participating in a universal, archetypal process can help you find your way through the creative wilderness. Journal about how the hero's journey relates to your own process.

Write a Letter to Your Project: If you get stuck on your creative journey, write a letter to your project. Use this prompt: *Dear Project, how can I move forward?* Write for ten minutes to see what emerges. Then, have the project write you back. What does it want **you** to know that you might be overlooking or even avoiding? This exercise allows for essential perspective-shifting that can help us return to the initial mission and vision we had for the project. It can be especially useful when we hit a wall—not only does it provide the potential insight to move forward, it can also show us that we already have the inner resources we need.

Take a Break: If you've lost your way, try stepping away from the project for a day, a week, or even longer. Let it incubate on the back burner of your mind and then return to it later, hopefully with fresh eyes and inspiration. It's impossible to remain constantly inspired and energized about a project; we all have our ebbs and flows in the creative journey. Counterintuitively, when we allow ourselves to step completely away to rest, we can then return with new energy and insight.

Reconnect: How can you recover the sense of play and experimentation that helped inspire your project initially? Try returning to your mission, vision, and values statements to remember your "why." Another way is to revisit your greatest inspirations, the ones that sparked your first creative interests, to reconnect to a sense of possibility. Or take a class to find a fresh perspective, which can help you return to beginner's mind.

Seek Outside Inspiration: Find a poem, visit a museum, or attend a concert to seek out inspiration from others who have found their way through to completion. Julia Cameron, in her book, *The Artist's Way,* frames this as "filling the well," emphasizing that we need plenty of fresh creative juice to do our own work. In this way, you build your reserves when you run dry. Remember, the creative process is a recursive one, and not all projects happen in a linear, straight-forward fashion. Seeking inspiration is a skillful way to restore your natural creative rhythm.

STAGE 3

Produce - Iteration, Collaboration, and Fruition

In our journey so far, we've explored the stages of Play and Plan, where we experiment with our ideas and map our process so we can take concrete action toward our creative goals. The groundwork we have laid so far culminates in Stage 3, Produce. In this stage we move into iteration, collaboration, and fruition, as we will discuss in the following three chapters.

Iteration is the process of refining our ideas and honing our works-in-process as we move toward completion. Collaboration is where we seek input, feedback, and assistance from others, which can offer synergy and fresh perspectives. Fruition is the process of completion, when we finish the work and share it with the world (if that is indeed our aspiration). Fruition also invites celebration and an acknowledgement of our accomplishments. Going back to the example of pottery, having first experimented with shape and form while the clay is wet, and shaping the pieces we intend to fire, we move into the actual glazing and firing process.

Here, the once-malleable clay becomes hardened into its final structure.

In Chapter 7, Iteration, we clarify how working through multiple versions empowers us to move closer to a finished product over time. We also discuss how stepping away allows us the necessary objectivity to improve the work. Additionally, we explore how feedback from peers and experts can improve the project as we build community and decrease the potential for creative isolation. The following graphic illustrates the iterative and interconnected nature of the creative process within the Syncreate model.

ITERATE TO CREATE

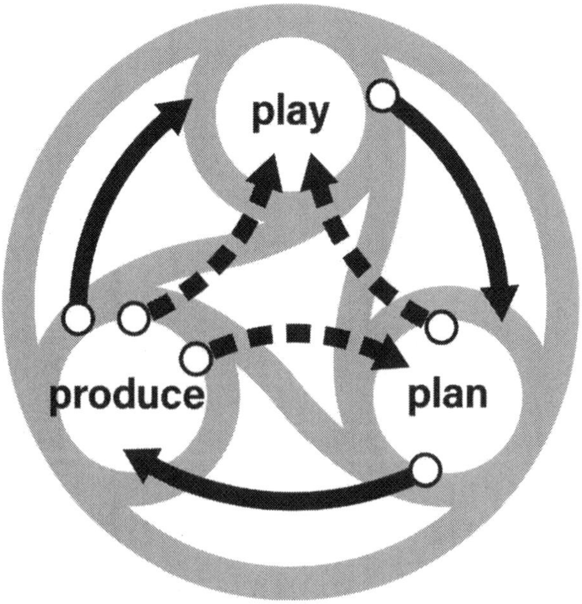

Chapter 8, Collaboration, explains how working with others can provide synergy and built-accountability. And in Chapter 9, Fruition, we encourage celebrating completion and examine how we bring our work to the larger world with dignity, gratitude, and interconnection. We also address the sometimes tricky relationship between art and entrepreneurship. In Stage 1, we emphasized the importance of play as it relates to the creative process. In the journey from idea to fruition, we need to embrace not-knowing in order to build a sense of the map we'll need. We also need to bridge the gap between our desires and our abilities, and we can do this through a variety of specific methods. The key in this stage is to catch our ideas by honoring them with attention, caretaking, and joyful study and experimentation.

CHAPTER SEVEN

ITERATION

Katherine Anne Porter (1890 – 1980) was an American journalist, essayist, short story writer, novelist, and political activist, and she was most well-known for Ship of Fools, *a best-selling novel published in 1962. Porter was born in Texas and much of her writing is set in Texas and Mexico. She won the Pulitzer in 1966 and the American Book Award and was appointed to the American Academy of Arts and Letters. Charlotte first read Porter's work in a community college writing class, taking great inspiration from her content, style and process. Porter apparently revised each of her stories upwards of sixty times before she was satisfied. Let's take a minute with that—sixty times? Rather than feeling oppressed by this number, we celebrate the patience and freedom this gives us as we close the gap between our aspirations and our abilities.*

We've arrived at the next stage, iteration: the process of creating, testing, and refining until we reach a satisfactory final product. First we create, and then we step back and evaluate. How close have we come to our desired result? What needs to be changed or modified? Could a radically different approach actually improve upon our original idea? Based on the answers to these questions, we hone our work until it is ready for the world. Contrary to popular conceptions about creativity, iteration is much more likely to get us where we want to be. An effective and strategic approach, iteration allows us to incrementally refine based on how the work-in-progress matches up to our initial vision, and allows us to incorporate the feedback we receive from the world. It reinforces the reality that we need other people to gain objectivity so that our work can grow into its full potential.

Iteration actually makes the creative process feel more accessible. It is rooted in the wisdom that multiple versions of a project (or product) are crucial. Used widely in the startup and technology world, iteration is a great concept to explore as it highlights the recursive nature of creativity. It is the principle behind rapid prototyping, lean innovation, agile software development, and design thinking. Any startup investor will want to know whether an idea or product has already been thoroughly tested, honed, and refined before backing it financially. We are not saying art is only about money, but we *are* saying that revision and feedback help close the gap between ideation and fruition. In Chapter 10, we dive deeper into these concepts as they apply to teams collaborating to solve complex creative problems.

The following image illustrates how the iterative nature of the creative process and iteration relates to the stages of Play, Plan, and Produce. When we reach a particular milestone, we can decide whether we are ready to move forward (thumbs up), or if we need to return to a previous stage (thumbs down).

FLEXIBLE TIMELINE

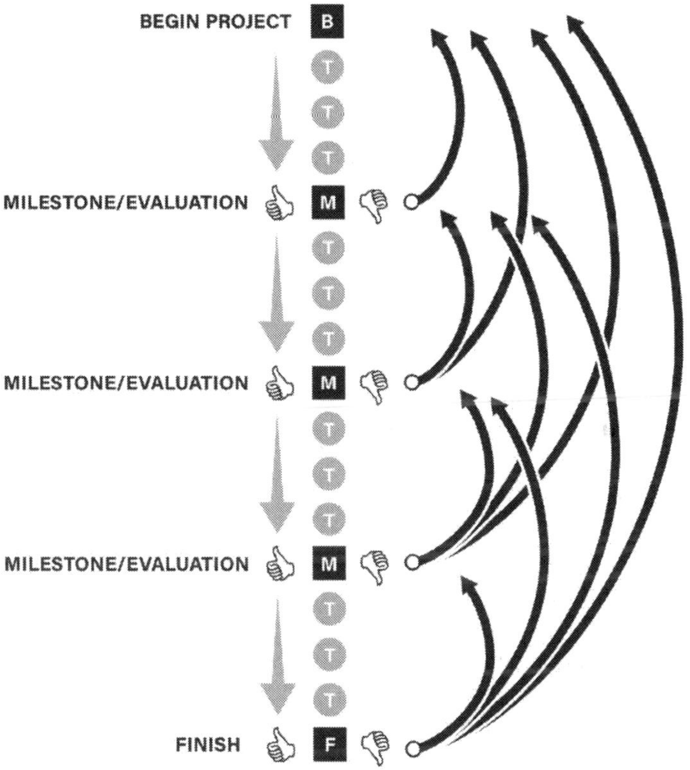

For folks new to the creative process, this stage can be somewhat elusive. Making multiple versions of a project might appear as non-inspired or an indication of our failed abilities. In our experiences working with students on their writing, we've observed their initial resistance toward the revision process; it is laborious and not always fun. However, when they end up with an award-winning essay or the surprising "A," their pride and satisfaction is a palpable validation of the process. It's a circular journey: we attempt to express our ideas, receive feedback or take time away to get objectivity, and then refine based on this insight. Iteration allows us the space both to measure how a given version matches our original vision or conversely, to let go of it in favor of something even better.

Getting Comfortable with Iteration

It's understandable to feel overwhelmed by too many ideas or to harbor fears about committing to a single idea for deep exploration. The excitement of all those possibilities can sometimes feel oppressive when it is time to focus. It's like a fear of commitment; we may feel that in choosing one road over another, we lose something in the process. However, by going deep with a single idea, we can actually tap into a reservoir of richness we might never have discovered by merely skimming the surface. Iteration is the means by which we can go deep; it allows us to play, refine, and complete. We get to play "what if" and see what new angles and dimensions emerge, which allows the project to evolve and take on more strength and power.

Our willingness to experiment, hone, and fine-tune leads to both a satisfying process and product. This might run counter to the (often unhelpful) notion of genius and single, instantaneous acts of creation. Instead, we encourage a commitment to working hard and playing with iteration, as this allows us to actually deliver on our ideas. This doesn't mean we have to give up on our other inspirations, but simply that we must focus on one thing at a given time (which does not preclude working on several different projects simultaneously). Poet and scholar Paula Gunn Allen put it this way: Think of your creative ideas as horses in the pen. You have to choose one and see where riding it will take you. And when you come back, all of those ideas/horses will be waiting for their turn.

Rehearsal/Revision/Fine-tuning

Once you've completed a working draft, it's time to hone and shape it into its final form which can require multiple iterations. When Melinda works with writers, she uses the analogy of a sculptor roughing out a block of marble, which is then ready for the finer work of shaping, sculpting, and fine-tuning. Writers must create their own raw materials in the form of a rough draft, which then requires multiple rounds of revision, editing, and proofreading before it is ready for publication. For musicians and actors, this is the rehearsal period. Performers will often play their songs both in practice and in live shows many times before committing them to a final recording. Likewise, stage actors spend months in rehearsal before bringing their work to a live audience.

If you study the creative process of successful musicians, writers, and artists, you will discover that most of them experimented with many different versions of their work before getting to the final version. One fiction writer Melinda worked with on a novel had a system set out for this iterative process; she would first create a plot draft, sketching out all the major plot points. Then she would rework the draft emphasizing character development, and then on her third revision she would focus on scene and setting. Subsequent drafts would fine-tune the use of language, phrasing, and sentence structure, etc. This is just one example of how to make a major project manageable with a series of smaller steps, using iteration to revise and refine along the way.

People sometimes say, "I'm no artist. I can't even draw a straight line." But, we can draw a crooked line. We can see where it isn't straight. We can use an eraser to remove crooked parts and then correct them to make the line straighter. These incremental adjustments can produce the straight line that we were unable to achieve on the first attempt. Iteration is the heart of the creative process. It shifts the thinking from "success vs. failure" to "trial and error"—from "it's not right" to "it's not right yet."

–Dreux Carpenter
Writer, Designer

Time Away

One way to gain objectivity on the work is to take some time away. This offers the opportunity to look at what we've created so far with a more dispassionate eye. You've probably heard more than one writer talking about putting a draft of a book away for six months to a year. This gives them some distance from what they've created, allowing for a new perspective when they return to it later. Time away from the project can also be an opportunity to purposefully engage in another project or return to an activity that evokes a sense of play. Some artists intentionally nurture more than one project at a time, both to gain objectivity and to ensure that they are always working on their craft. This has at least two positive results: 1) they are honing their overall skill in their chosen artistic field, and 2) they are acquiring the necessary distance to return to the first project with a clearer perspective of what's working and what needs improving.

Feedback

Once you have a solid work-in-progress, it's a good time to start getting feedback from trusted peers and colleagues. Be selective in who you ask for input, and initially only request it from a few people whose opinions and judgments you really value. Then you can incorporate the feedback into further iterations and revisions (as you find it helpful) until you arrive at a more complete version. When you have diligently honed multiple versions to arrive at a more complete project, we then recommend seeking another round of feedback from experts. This could include established professionals such as literary agents and reviewers, producers, etc., who can help move the work toward its final fruition and presentation to the public.

Marking the Milestones

Don't forget to honor each milestone you've achieved along the way. Take a moment to reflect upon your creative process and acknowledge how far you've come. Find ways to celebrate that are meaningful to you, whether it be a special dinner with friends and family, or a weekend getaway, or simply a well-deserved walk in nature. Many creatives get so focused on moving through the stages of production that they forget to enjoy the small victories and accomplishments along the way. These milestones are actually quite meaningful—they provide the opportunity to reflect on and acknowledge our progress, which can positively shift our relationship to the creative process.

Toggling Between Convergent and Divergent Thinking

When working with multiple iterations, it can be helpful to consider how the two types of thinking might be used with more strategic agility. Perhaps a given version needs some fresh energy or broadening of scope, and this when the playful, specific use of divergent thinking is appropriate. For example:

- What if I changed the point-of-view?
- What if I introduced a different element into the project?
- Could I start in a different place?
- How could I collaborate?

These kinds of questions can help enliven the project with new possibilities.

On the other hand, perhaps the project needs more tightening or weaving together of disparate elements. If so, harnessing the power of convergent thinking could yield the next, stronger and more impactful version. For example:

- Can something be cut?
- What if I combined characters?
- Am I trying to do too much in one piece?
- What is the minimum needed to convey the message?

For example, a writing client of Melinda's was struggling to draft concise chapter synopses for her novel. She asked how long they should be: a page or two each? "Too much!" Melinda thought; they should be more succinct. But how to skillfully convey this much-needed pivot to the client? In the end, she challenged her to keep each synopsis to one paragraph, or even to try writing them as haiku poems. The client embraced this latter approach, crafting a simple haiku for each chapter, which freed her up immensely and allowed her to focus on the most important themes. This unusual approach combined both convergent and divergent thinking, yielding something both fresh and precise.

As we approach the complete version of the work, we must inevitably begin to converge more and more until it reaches its final form. Along the way, we've played with iterations, we've asked for feedback, and we've marked the milestones that indicated we are making progress. In short, the creative journey has required us to be both flexible and persistent in our quest toward fruition.

The following image offers another perspective on how iteration fits into the Syncreate model of Play, Plan, and Produce:

ITERATIVE PROCESS

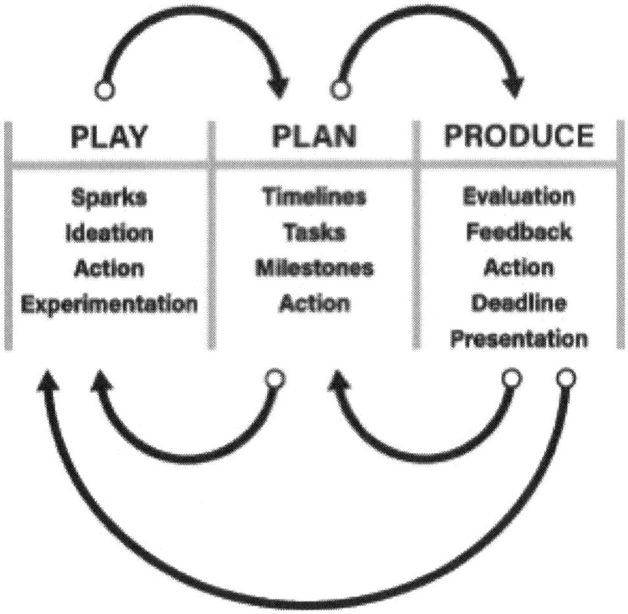

Creative Sparks for Iteration

Focus on One Area: Identify an area of the project you think needs work, and ask yourself—can this get stronger? Pick one element to focus on and try developing it further. Maybe one of your characters takes an unexpected turn, or you introduce a key change into the song, or re-work that broken piece of clay into something new.

Cultivate Feedback: Ask a friend or colleague for feedback on your work in progress. We need feedback from trusted individuals who understand the delicate nature of the role; they offer us tactful guidance as to the clarity and impact of our project. These are folks who stand alongside us and say, "Yes, I see where you're trying to go and this is how you might course-correct in order to get there."

Pivot: Change the genre of the work or experiment with translating it into a different medium. For example, if you've written a screenplay, try writing it as a haiku or sonnet. See what insights or understandings emerge. This may open up a new doorway, changing the direction of the work completely or transforming it into a mixed-media piece. Or maybe it will simply give you new ideas for further development in the existing medium.

Implement Strategic Change: Alter one component of the work in some significant way and see how it changes the overall effect. For example, if you're composing a song, change the tempo or rhythm. This approach deepens our intimacy with our project—by exploring changes, we are deepening our understanding of what works and what doesn't work. As creators, we must become the experts of our own material. Notice how the word "author" is nestled into the word "authority." In writing, the author must become the authority on the project, with a thorough knowledge of its different iterations, in order to make the most informed choice concerning its best outcome.

Embrace a Lower Standard: If some aspect of the project needs improvement but you're not sure how to proceed, allow yourself to be actively "bad" at noodling around with it. This can remove the pressure or anxiety we might feel about immediately getting it right. You could try sketching out some ideas with your non-dominant hand, for example, or creating a model out of crumpled up paper or found objects or whatever junk you happen to have around. Experimenting in this way can yield unexpected insights. Sometimes surrendering to imperfection is the best way forward.

CHAPTER EIGHT

THE POWER OF COLLABORATION

This book, and all of our work together with Syncreate, is the product of collaboration. When we first connected, we discovered a synergy that allowed us to create more together than either could have done independently. We also realized that our collaboration enhanced both our inspiration and movement toward completion. During our meetings we discussed ideas and implemented action plans with remarkable speed, building upon our collaborative energy.

When we decided to write this book, we wanted to share our ideas and approaches to the creative process. However, we both lead full lives and it was hard to imagine when we would actually be able to sit down and write. The only dedicated time we had together was the two hours of our weekly meetings, so Melinda suggested we take that time for our writing sessions, which has been a highly efficient way to realistically achieve the smaller milestones needed to complete the book. Over the course of the initial pandemic year, we continued to meet virtually to work on our revision and successfully completed the book, a testament to the power of collaboration and incremental progress.

In the most basic sense, collaboration involves two or more people working together on a project. There are many good reasons to collaborate, and it's helpful to know when to collaborate versus when to work independently. Collaboration empowers us to accomplish more by working with others, as an often-quoted proverb goes: "If you want to go fast, go alone. If you want to go far, go together." While we may be able to do many wonderful things on our own, when we work together with others, we develop synergy, while pooling our ideas, inspirations, and resources.

According to creativity researcher and consultant Keith Sawyer, "Collaboration is the secret to breakthrough creativity." Indeed, research shows that diverse teams yield more potentially useful ideas, leading to greater creativity and innovation. Used strategically, collaboration allows us to amplify the power of our individual work. A drawback of collaboration is that it can sometimes lead either to conflict, when people cannot agree, or the tendency toward "groupthink." Here, people tend to concur out of politeness rather than engaging in productive critique. The key is to balance individual work with active collaboration, knowing when to divide and conquer and when to work together simultaneously.

This is the strategy we have used to write this book. A typical collaboration day for us began with a phone call to determine how we would split up our time together. We discussed who would work on which section of the manuscript, and then we worked independently on different chapters for

20-minute blocks of time. At the end of our timed writing, we got back on the phone to review our progress. Normally we would do this together in person, but the pandemic forced us to get creative, as it were, with our use of time and technology. We actually found that we were able to accomplish a lot this way in a very concentrated amount of time.

As an aspiring artist, I found Syncreate to be a valuable experience that inspired me to continue with my work. I'm a woman who delights in creating jewelry. The process, however, can feel lonely at times. In those moments, thoughts can creep in which create doubt about my abilities and vision. Mingling with other creatives, and listening to their own challenges has helped me to push past my fears. I have met so many amazing artists, and have even found a few collaborative partners! I have felt less lonely and doubtful by connecting with the community through this wonderful group. I always walk away from each meeting with inspiration and renewed energy!

—Sabzeh Nakhchi
Designer and Jewelry Artist
Instagram: @sabzehjewelry

Synergy and Collaboration

We find many examples throughout the creative world of how team effort strengthens the artistic process. Many musicians only improve their skills by playing with other people; they can accelerate their prowess more quickly and profoundly than if they only practiced by themselves. Successful screenwriters also often collaborate. If you study the careers of Chris Markus and Stephen McFeely, (*The Chronicles of Narnia* film franchise, *The First Avenger, The Winter Soldier* and *Civil War, Thor: The Dark World, Avengers: Infinity War* and *Avengers: Endgame*), you'll see the impact of concentrated, collaborative work. If you're familiar with the The Cornetto Trilogy *(Hot Fuzz, Shaun of the Dead, The World's End*), you already know Simon Pegg and Edgar Wright's wit and unique perspective make for compelling storytelling.

In instances of collaboration, two people working on a project together bring twice the amount of motivation and determination—and if one's interest or commitment wanes, that's only 50% of the energy being depleted. In contrast, if we are working alone and lose our way or we feel defeated—that's 100% of the energy compromised.

Cooperation breaks up the isolation we might feel when working alone. Collaboration can also result in stronger drafts and therefore stronger final products since there are two sets of eyes on the material. Because each person brings a unique perspective and set of ideas, the combined focus of two or more people offers the possibility of creative synergy.

You may ask: what is synergy and how is it different from or complementary to collaboration? According to *Oxford Learner's Dictionary*, synergy is "the extra energy, power, success . . . achieved by two or more people or companies working together, instead of on their own." Synergy goes beyond the simple act of cooperating with others to get something done; it's more of a dialectical process where the tension of opposites or the creative energies of two or more people combine to yield something new, different, and greater than any one of them could have produced working alone.

Accountability and Communication

Another boon of creative partnership is built-in accountability. By committing to small goals, each partner accepts their individual responsibility for moving the project forward, which provides additional extrinsic motivation. Doing so builds mutual trust and engagement. Clear expectations are also necessary for an effective partnership. Collaborators must communicate their needs and desires for the project's direction, and plan for regular check-ins to ensure the success and well-being of all involved. Having flexibility around the agreed-upon milestones is likewise helpful—keeping the end-point in focus allows more ebb and flow when it comes to adjusting the micro goals and milestones along the way.

For example, in our drafting of this book, we made the commitment to complete a first draft within nine months. We kept this goal in mind while adjusting to and accommodating our very different and busy schedules. Not all partnerships need to look like this: some collaborators choose to work independently and then combine their efforts, while others find different ways of dividing and combining their labor. We know that collaboration is not realistic for every person or every project, but we also know the satisfaction and joy of reaching our goals and the ways accountability expands our thinking and our possibilities.

Creative Sparks for Collaboration

Delegate and Accelerate: Find ways to delegate the labor of production for maximum efficiency. This way, each person makes a meaningful contribution based on individual strengths and skill sets, while still feeling part of a team. As we described earlier in the chapter, we used this technique when drafting this book. We actually found this to be an incredibly efficient and productive way to work under less-than-ideal circumstances. Harness the power of delegation to accelerate your projects.

Plan a Working Retreat: Set aside a three-day period for collaboration. This could be a short retreat or a series of content generation sessions that give focused attention to the project. Making the decision to prioritize the collaboration can yield fruitful results. Such sessions bring the project into sharp focus and create a sense of accomplishment. These concentrated work periods also deepen the partnership to accelerate convergence—you are literally coming together to help a project coalesce.

Accountability Check-In: Begin your collaboration sessions with an update, where each individual reports on their progress. This way, everyone learns the current status of the project, including items completed and in progress. It can also be helpful to use collaboration apps for virtual accountability updates.

Foster Connections: Share your progress on individual creative projects outside of the formal collaboration, including milestones, challenges, and celebrations. In our experience, a five-minute sharing from each collaborator strengthens our sense of connection. This in turn builds the empathy, trust, and confidence necessary to meaningful partnership. Also, interesting synergies may arise when partners share experiences with personal efforts and inspirations, which can also inform the collaboration.

Share Sustenance: Get together for a meal with your collaborators or plan some other type of creative outing where you can commune, feed your bodies and souls, and share inspirations. Positive rapport breeds creative collaboration. Spend time cultivating it outside of official "work time." Nourishment comes in many forms, both literally and metaphorically.

CHAPTER NINE

FRUITION

Melinda recorded and released her first album of original music in New Orleans in 2004. To celebrate this milestone, she organized a CD-release party with her band and invited friends and family, many of whom came from all over the country for the event. It was the first time her parents (divorced since she was 13 years old) had been in the same room together since her college graduation. She rented an event space above a popular bar in New Orleans' Warehouse District and threw a big party and jam session embracing community and creativity. Based on the success of the record launch, she felt the energy and inspiration to play more gigs both locally and regionally, apply to music festivals and conferences, and begin touring nationally, even in the aftermath of Hurricane Katrina the following year.

Now that the project is complete, it's time to celebrate and share it. For some, this can be a fun and exciting process, but for others it can activate anxiety and self-doubt. How will people respond? Will they appreciate it? What will the reviewers say? Will it sell? Bringing our creative work into the public eye can be both incredibly gratifying and immensely triggering. Many of us must also grapple with the business side of creativity at this point. This chapter considers the fruition stage of the creative process, including completion, celebration, gratitude and giving back.

Embracing the Process

It's natural to yearn for fruition—the long-awaited moment when all our efforts result in a final polished work. However, because we are surrounded by such final products, focusing on completion can also shortcut the joys and discoveries of the creative process itself. Too much focus on the end goal early on can rob us of fully experiencing the journey toward our destination. Embracing process, as much as product, helps us create balance in our artistic lives.

We need to live into our art, develop an intimate relationship with it, and embrace the practice of making it. If we only focus on the product, we may short-circuit the full experience of engaging with our creative impulses. As Mensah Demary suggests, you must "find absolute satisfaction in your daily work as an artist, supremely vital to your being: Without it, you will never be satisfied with the result." Consistently practicing our art form liberates and fulfills us, helping us along the path toward completion.

Reflection

The fruition stage is also an excellent time to reflect back on our process as a whole, from ideation to completion, noting our challenges and obstacles as well as our moments of growth and success. This helps us to develop more self-awareness around our creative habits in order to further refine them going forward. Understanding our own best practices for creative production means we won't have to reinvent the wheel each time we embark on a new project. It also allows us to learn from our previous mistakes and avoid similar pitfalls in the future. When Charlotte writes nonfiction essays, she keeps a running journal of tasks, so she can map out the stages of her process. When an essay is accepted for publication, she spends time writing about ***how*** she wrote the piece, so she knows how to repeat the process. Another important avenue for reflection is to consider the people who have helped us along the way, underscoring that creativity isn't merely a solo venture.

Self-Doubt

As important as it is to celebrate our accomplishments, the fruition stage can also provoke anxiety and self-doubt as we prepare to share our work with the world in the form of publication, performance, or launch. Many of us feel perfectly content alone in the studio but terrified of the gallery opening where we become the center of attention. This is an odd paradox of the creative process, particularly for introverts; we don't necessarily enjoy being in the public eye. It can be helpful at these times to return again to the original inspiration for our creative work. While many of us may create purely for personal expression, therapeutic catharsis, and joy, many also yearn to share our ideas with the world, which can be a powerful driver toward completion. Reconnecting with this desire can help us navigate the rapids of self-doubt around bringing our creations to the light of day.

For many of us, self-doubt and imposter syndrome make us question ourselves, especially when we want to celebrate a moment of progress. We might observe someone else's finished work or hear them talk with such confidence about their project, making us question our right to mark our own milestones. Rest assured, it is quite common to feel misgivings about ourselves at every point in the creative process—and the antidote is to focus on incremental progress. If we show up regularly and celebrate our individual growth, we can overcome our hesitations.

Art and Entrepreneurship

Gone are the days, for most of us anyway, where we simply get to create and then pass off the business and marketing to a record label or big-name publisher or art dealer. The vast majority of contemporary creatives fall into the category of independent musicians, self-publishers, and artist-entrepreneurs. Yet, we may also carry a deep ambivalence about self-promotion and the notion of "selling out." Others may be naturally adept at networking, talking about our creative work, or promoting ourselves on social media. While we don't have to become something we're not, learning to engage with the public about our work is increasingly important. Connecting with other artists and sharing our process can yield growth and insight as well as building awareness of our work. Experiment with how to tell your story in the most authentic way.

From our work with entrepreneurs and startups, we have realized that creativity and entrepreneurship are actually closely related. Entrepreneurship is an inherently creative process that involves each of the stages we've discussed throughout the book: Plan, Play, and Produce. If you're curious to learn more about the process of experimentation and iteration that many startups employ, we recommend the book *The Lean Startup* by Eric Ries. Understanding entrepreneurship through the lens of creativity can help us embrace the business side of sharing our work with the world.

Celebration

So, you've done it—after spending hours developing your craft, living inside the imprecise journey of creation, receiving peer-level and professional feedback, you've arrived at the final product: Congratulations! This is a delicious moment to savor the effort and growth you've devoted to completing the project. It's a tremendous accomplishment, and we highly encourage you to rejoice in this arrival.

Fruition represents the culmination of any creative journey. It can also be a stepping stone to launching or releasing the work out into the world, if that is the intention. As we've discussed in the preceding chapters, we encounter many challenges and roadblocks along the way. In view of the often-solitary nature of creativity, honoring our accomplishments with a ritual or celebration helps us to acknowledge their reality. For example, after the long months of working largely in isolation, Melinda celebrated the successful defense of her doctoral dissertation with a group of friends at a local patio bar. Another approach is self care as celebration; Charlotte often gets a massage as a way of nurturing herself to mark a milestone. Honoring the moment of fruition in this way also allows us to share our progress, launch the work into the world, and potentially inspire others to embark on their own creative journeys.

Consider the function of graduation ceremonies in our lives: When a student completes a certain level of education, we celebrate that hard work and completion through a formal ritual. Think about the fruition of your project with the same kind of significance. With such a celebration, we mark a rite of passage and share that moment with others. We encourage you to think about the specific, authentic ways you will savor this moment. Plan a party: This can range from the simple to the extravagant—from a potluck at a local park to an all-out bash. However you decide to celebrate, mark the occasion for yourself. Perhaps the celebration includes a creative showcase of others' work as well as your own, or a crowdsourcing event to help others find connections and support for their projects. This coming together of people and energies is how we affirm life: art allows us to connect and weave ourselves into the fabric of humanity.

Melinda and Charlotte have poured their vast experience and expertise into Syncreate. I've had the wonderful opportunity to work with them in person and am thrilled to know that their insights will spark creativity in countless others. Now that their project is realized as a book, people all over the world can learn how to tap into their creativity to unleash so much of their hidden potential.

—Patricia Hagen
Design Coach and Mental Health Advocate
https://www.linkedin.com/in/patricia-hagen/
Instagram: @patkat

Gratitude

No creative journey is completed in isolation. Cultivating gratitude for everything that makes our creative work possible keeps us grounded and focused on the positive. Even if we're locked in a painting studio for a week, we could give thanks for the brushes, the canvases, and the people who made them. Remember the people who have believed in us or inspired us to begin in the first place, and supported us along the way. Our work is made possible by a whole chain of people and events; remembering this keeps us centered and adds a deeper sense of value and interconnection to our creations.

Contributing to the Creative Community

The fruition stage is also a time to think about giving back; it's an opportunity to build community and to deepen our connection with others. You might consider three actions to take on behalf of others when you complete your project. Some examples could include: gifting a friend a master class to help them develop their craft; funding three hours of studio time for a fellow musician; or volunteering at a local arts organization. Giving back to our community is one way we can illuminate the seemingly invisible creative process. Aspiring to support others in their journey can also help to sustain us when we feel like giving up. In addition, extending ourselves in this way helps us frame a new story about what it means to be an artist; rather than the tale of the inherently gifted, solitary genius, we craft a more accurate narrative emphasizing that good work takes time, patience, practice, and community.

Creative Sparks for Fruition

Reflect on How Far You've Traveled: Once you finish a project, take a quiet moment to reflect on the journey you have just completed and to honor your efforts. Take some time to chronicle the incremental steps from the initial inspiration to the final product. Acknowledge the creative labor you have put in along the way and appreciate your own hard work.

Revisit the Map and Action Plan: Return to the milestone map you outlined at the project's beginning. Note what worked well and what felt challenging. What deadlines did you meet or not meet? What unexpected obstacles or synchronicities did you encounter along the way, and how did you work with them? What tools, processes, or practices were most helpful to you in achieving your creative goals? By tracking your creative process in this way, you can develop a set of best practices to intentionally incorporate into future projects.

Plan a Celebration: Whether it is a book signing, record-release party, or gallery opening, invite your colleagues and loved ones to celebrate your efforts. Let people know how important this milestone is for you and allow yourself to receive and embrace their support and encouragement. Like any kind of ritual or ceremony, this act of celebration helps us mentally and emotionally cross the finish line of our creative marathons.

Find Ways to Give Back: Identify three things you will do once the project is complete to support your creative community (volunteer at or donate to an arts-organization, offer a free workshop on your creative medium, or mentor a young artist). By committing to helping others in this way, you begin to move beyond your individual pursuits and into a space of interconnection where you embrace a larger community. It can also refill the well of inspiration when you feel stuck or disengaged from your own work.

Mentor Others: Once you have completed a particular creative journey, commit to mentoring and/or providing accountability partnership to someone else. Share what you have learned, both the challenges and the successes. Creativity is so often a solitary process with few tangible elements to share before the final completion. Thus it can be extremely helpful to others in the midst of a process to have their journey witnessed, to feel seen and heard when they are experiencing a block or breakthrough. The journey becomes both more satisfying and fruitful when you can share it with others and vice-versa.

CHAPTER TEN

TEAMS AND THE SYNCREATE PROCESS

We often begin our Syncreate team meetings with personal check-ins and then share progress updates about our individual creative work outside of our formal collaborative projects. This allows us to renew our connection to one another on both a personal and creative level, which helps to lay the groundwork for the meeting itself. Knowing that positive rapport, trust, and authentic communication are vital to collaboration, we value this time for creative exchange. Reaffirming our relationships in this way supports and enhances our synergy. With this personal foundation in place, we then move into the formal business of our work meetings. Similarly, when we facilitate creative gatherings for groups that don't know each other, we begin by asking people to say a bit about their own creative work and their inspiration for attending. We are always delighted by how quickly this kind of sharing leads to a sense of connection among the group that leads to risk-taking and deeper creative growth.

Having explored the stages of Play, Plan, and Produce throughout the book, we now turn our attention to how teams can move through the creative process together. We touched on some of these ideas in Chapter 8: The Power of Collaboration, in the context of personal creative partnerships, and here we focus on how organizational teams and work groups can collectively harness the creative process to:

- Collaborate effectively
- Build relationships, communication, and trust
- Maximize design time
- Utilize resources in the most efficient manner

Understanding these principles allows for a more humanist approach to collective creativity, rooted in a value system that honors the time, space, and support required for true problem solving and innovation in service of the greater good as well as the bottom line. We can drive connection and insight by strategically building nimble teams based on the unique skills of their members, tailored to the specific needs of the given project. In other words, not every team member needs to be on every project; instead, we can match skill sets with project goals in an agile and real-time fashion. Additionally, knowing how to utilize divergence and convergence when working as a team can help build momentum and heighten impact.

Idea Generation and Team Creativity

When working in teams, we must foster the conditions that allow for rich explorations of idea generation. In the Syncreate model, we call this Play or divergence. Effective brainstorming builds upon the collective strengths of the team. This exciting step in the creative process allows us to be bold, dream big, and to depart from familiar and known ways of viewing a challenge. Often (but not always) when we embark on idea generation with a group, our individual thinking is bolstered, challenged, and expanded. Under the right conditions, we might even call this accelerated thinking, as new ideas beget new ideas. Team idea generation also reveals how exploring ideas with others enhances our individual creative thinking and projects.

Researchers focusing on organizational creativity have found that the best solutions arrive when a team clearly defines and frames the challenge in front of them. So before moving to creative ideation and brainstorming, ask each team member to individually write down, in their own words, the problem the group is collectively trying to solve. Once everyone has written down their statements, ask them to share using a whiteboard. Note areas of overlap and differences: What terms and concepts are people using to define the problem? What different perspectives are showing up that could be helpful to the project goals? Once all the definitions have been added, is anything still missing? Now, try distilling this collective wisdom down to a clear and concise statement of the problem at hand.

Once the team has clearly defined the problem, they can begin to identify potential solutions. However, It's essential to understand how, when, and why true idea generation and brainstorming works. Otherwise this step can actually become counterproductive, leading to groupthink and leaving some team members feeling disengaged. Groupthink is the phenomenon of converging too quickly on one idea to the exclusion of other potentially useful solutions. Fortunately, specific brainstorming techniques and guidelines exist to help avoid these pitfalls and encourage respectful dissent and robust dialogue. When team members have clear and defined parameters, they can be more comfortable in taking greater leaps with their ideas and insights. In this way, structured brainstorming (described in more detail in the Creative Sparks at the end of the chapter) provides clarity regarding when to diverge and converge, enhancing creative ideation and individual risk-taking.

Trust and Communication

Another important component of effective teams involves balancing positive rapport and connection with healthy disagreement and critical feedback. This can be challenging, especially when we aim to build diverse teams. However, extensive research on effective teams conducted by Google and other researchers reveals the vital importance of psychological safety and trust for teams to work productively. In addition, assembling a wide array of perspectives and expertise gives the team a broader range of experiences and potential ideas to work with. This expands the pool of possibilities, which can create dissonance among the team, but which can also generate a kind of productive tension that amplifies true creativity and innovation.

With a healthy, diverse team in place, along with definitive processes for idea generation, leaders must also clearly define the team's purpose and intentions. Articulating the vision, goals, and a path to meaningful collaboration allows the team to work together effectively. Without this clarity of purpose, the team can aimlessly flounder, attempting to generate ideas without understanding their collective "why." For more on this, explore Melinda's book *A Mindful Approach to Team Creativity and Collaboration in Organizations* and Brené Brown's *Dare to Lead*. This is also an opportune time to revisit the organization's core values and mission to ensure that new ideas are rooted in foundational goals.

Covid-19 has forced us to all to re-evaluate how we can effectively build engagement, connection, and trust in teams. Whether we were ready or not we were forced to innovate to adapt and survive. As organizations continue to transition to the post-Covid new norm, this book can be used as a practical research-based roadmap to step up to the challenge. The easy-to-follow model to unleash innovation and collaboration (Play, Plan, Produce) will no doubt have a profound and lasting impact on the teams that put them into practice! I'm looking forward to using it with my own team and the client teams I work with!

—Michelle Poole, PCC, PHR
CEO, Coaching 4 Good
www.coaching4good.com

Teams and Idea Evaluation

As we've described, creating the conditions for effective idea generation requires strategic understanding of the creative process. Diligently observing these steps creates the foundation for the next stage: idea evaluation. Like idea generation, this step requires a balance of open, honest, and authentic dialogue along with clear protocols, including productive feedback and action planning. During idea evaluation, falling within the Plan or convergence stage of the Syncreate model, the team approach can really shine. Once a number of different possibilities have been put forward using idea generation techniques, teams must then evaluate which ones have the best potential for further development. We include specific guidelines for idea evaluation at the end of the chapter.

Teams and Production

Having generated, evaluated, and refined our ideas, it's time to move into concrete action, into the third phase of the Syncreate approach, Produce. In the business and design worlds, this stage of the creative process involves prototyping and iteration, which means testing out our ideas, soliciting feedback, and refining them until they are fully realized. The terms lean innovation, agile product development, and design thinking all reference this process in the context of organizational innovation. In the startup environment, this may include presenting an idea or prototype to potential investors. This requires developing a working model and refining it into a "minimum viable product" validated through customer experience and feedback. A great example of this in the context of the pandemic was the rush to develop and implement testing, treatment, and effective vaccines.

Teams and Accountability

As with individual creative work, accountability is a potent and necessary element of successful teamwork. It is extremely important to clarify goals, deadlines, and accountability measures before divvying up tasks. In other words, make sure everyone has the same understanding of ideas and expectations. Teams can also circumvent problems and tension by taking the time to establish routine check-ins and agreed-upon protocols for accountability. Reporting back to the larger group concerning individual responsibilities provides an anchor for team members to commit to their roles. This allows each person to successfully function autonomously, with the freedom to do things in their own way, something essential for maximizing creativity in team settings.

In order to maximize team collaboration and accountability, it's important to follow four steps:

1) Identify the major goals and milestones required to complete a specific project
2) Break these goals and milestones into smaller, incremental tasks
3) Assign roles according to individuals' strengths and unique skill sets
4) Establish regular check-ins for updates and adjustments

Following these guidelines offers clarity to individual team members regarding expectations and deadlines for effective collaboration. In this way, teams can consciously utilize divergence and convergence, with individuals coming together to explore idea generation and then working independently on their individual responsibilities with periodic check-ins.

As you can see, working in teams presents unique challenges and opportunities in the creative process. Following the guidelines presented in this chapter can both heighten personal connection and amplify the collaboration. The following list of creative sparks is designed to support teams working through the stages of Play, Plan, and Produce, as described throughout the book so far.

Creative Sparks for Working in Teams

Problem Framing and Definition: When collaborating with a group on a specific project or challenge, take time at the beginning of the process to clearly define the problem at hand. Intentionally framing the problem together as a group will greatly enhance the idea generation and brainstorming process, leading to better solutions. Ask each team member to describe the problem, in their own terms, and then compare the definitions. Note areas of overlap and difference, and pool this collective wisdom to create a concrete statement of the problem you're trying to solve.

Play - Idea Generation and Group Brainstorming: Having clearly defined the problem, you can then employ group brainstorming techniques, which work best when following a clear structure. Write the problem statement up on a whiteboard and invite everyone to reflect on it, individually writing down possible ideas or solutions. Then invite each person to share the results of their individual brainstorming on the whiteboard, noting common themes as well as outliers. Consider all possibilities rather than immediately dismissing ideas that may seem outlandish or "impossible." Some of the greatest innovations may have initially seemed impractical or outside the realm of feasibility.

Plan - Idea Evaluation: When it comes to idea evaluation, we are moving into convergence. In this stage, we examine the possibilities through a variety of lenses: Which idea best addresses your original challenge? Can you combine ideas for a more elegant solution? What is most resonant with your mission, vision, and values? List out the possibilities and ask each team member to vote on their top three choices for implementation. This will reveal areas of consensus and also allow for productive discussion of which solutions make the most sense in terms of organizational priorities and resources.

Produce - Rapid Prototyping and Refining: Once the group has identified a solution to explore, set a specific deadline for an initial design or mock-up. This quick creation and feedback loop is known as rapid prototyping, and it is an effective means for a team to understand if their ideas are feasible, practical, and (in the startup world) worthy of funding from potential investors. Seeking outside, expert opinions can provide additional insights to streamline the overall process. Additionally, this circular strategy of iteration and refinement empowers teams with potent opportunities to distill and clarify ideas, which reduces the time gap between idea generation and fruition.

Communication & Accountability: Set up a brief weekly accountability check-in with your team for quick updates on what each person is working on and where the project stands as a whole. In addition to specific processes, apps, or software you may be using for project tracking, regular check-ins are extremely helpful for building and maintaining relationships. They also give the process a more personal element that can minimize potentially costly miscommunications and misunderstandings.

CHAPTER ELEVEN

COMMUNITIES AND THE SYNCREATE PROCESS

Over the years, we've hosted a series of gatherings, workshops, and events in and around the Austin, Texas area focusing on the creative process. Through these offerings, we've come to meet a wide range of artists. Each occasion became an opportunity to affirm the importance of community. With these events, we've experimented with a number of exercises and facilitated many rich discussions about creativity. These conversations have revealed the common obstacles and inspirations of individual artists. We've gained great insight into group process and mutual accountability. In this chapter, we highlight our observations on the power of creative community.

Community is an essential aspect of the creative process. We discussed in Chapter 10 how enhanced communication and trust can benefit teams. Likewise, communities working together can artfully design their collaboration. Even our Syncreate logo, conveying circles within circles, symbolizes the importance of community. If we engage with others trying to foster creativity, we are more likely to connect, support, and commit to our own ideas.

In fact, by weaving this sense of engagement with community throughout our lives, we both fortify our resolve and build creative solidarity with others. Connecting with other creatives also allows for potent cross-pollination. For example, during one of our Syncreate community meetings, a young painter expressed her uncertainty about using social media. When another participant described how she made process videos on Instagram focused on her calligraphy, it created a lightning bolt moment: The painter then knew exactly what to do. At our next meeting, she was thrilled to report on developing her own process videos. In this way, connecting with others can be an important waypoint toward a joyful and productive creative process.

With the intention of supporting community, we design our events around three simple steps:

1) Introductions and updates
2) Creativity exercise
3) Goals and accountability

Beginning with introductions and updates, we invite participants to establish themselves as creatives, asking them to share their names and creative media in a sentence or two, often beginning with "I create . . . ." This simple statement can actually be a radical act of affirmation for those struggling with their "right" to claim a creative identity. We then invite attendees to share their challenges and triumphs around their projects. These shared moments validate that creativity is mostly a process, long before it is a product.

We then introduce an activity, asking participants to engage in a creative exercise that varies from meeting to meeting. These activities can range from the internal (a guided meditation) to the expressive (a drawing or writing exercise), to the communal (collaborative art-making with found objects). We have found that exploring a specific prompt in a group context can provide a rich occasion for simultaneous engagement with important restorative and inspirational value. At the end of the exercise, we invite people to share their discoveries and creations, which often yields mutual delight and insight. This in turn builds the confidence for each person to return to their individual projects with renewed commitment and resolve.

We conclude by asking each participant to commit to one or more tasks to complete within the next month. Breaking goals into small, incremental steps, and voicing our plans to others, can create a powerful sense of momentum. Some examples include: "I will clean off my writer's desk," or "I will order the paints I've wanted for two years." These micro moments of articulated action contain larger, and sometimes buried, dreams. In naming them, we free ourselves into actualized possibilities.

Creative Hygiene in Community

While we may take our creative energy and inspiration for granted, it actually requires care and cultivation. Indeed, we must "attend" to it as we do the other elements of basic living: nutrition, sleep, fitness, spirituality, financial stability/security, and so on. It can feel vulnerable to go outside our comfort zones and reach out to others for accountability, but the benefits outweigh the discomfort. Again, and again, participants have shared with us, "I almost didn't come tonight but I am so glad I did."

We may feel resistance towards this type of communal creative hygiene. This resistance can hold us back. A common misguided narrative suggests that "real" creatives don't need other people, which in most cases couldn't be further from the truth. While solitude is important in order to focus and hone our abilities, we can also benefit, and maybe even shine, as a result of spending intentional time with other artists.

The creative process can be elusive at times, at least for me. Going in and out of inspiration, and at other times, low motivation, can be a challenge. I attended Syncreate groups, where several artists of varying mediums came together to share their stories, and to receive feedback, and advice from fellow artists. I found my inspiration, and was motivated by Melinda to not just "go create something," but was encouraged to find my inner muse. I committed to creating a specific item, then came to the next meet-up with the electric charge of the creative collective under my wing. I recommend the Syncreate group to anyone looking for guidance into their own creative process, or simply curious about the creative process itself. My big take away from my experience: What I create, ends up creating ME.

—Tammy Cowen
Instagram: @Tashipics

Creative Citizenship

Supporting the creative endeavors of our wider community is one powerful mechanism available to us to engage in creative citizenship. Undeniably, we are not alone in our own artistic worlds. Rather, we move within a hive of creatives who support, nourish, and celebrate one another instead of competing and undercutting one another. As we discussed earlier in the book, this is where our accountability partners and faith tenders play a vital role in our artistic journeys. It's how we can both support others in their process and build a larger, more robust creative community. Like the other ways we engage in citizenship, we can choose to participate and contribute to the culture we want to create.

Creative Sparks for Cultivating Community

Facilitate a Creative Gathering: Plan a get-together to foster community and connection around creativity. Ask participants to introduce themselves and speak a little bit about their creative work. Lead a discussion of people's biggest challenges and inspirations. You can then create an accountability group to support each other in meeting creative goals.

Host a Creative Salon: Invite a group of artists to an event in which each person brings a piece of their work to share with the group. Ask the presenters to detail their creative process leading up to the finished work in order to illuminate each person's creative journey.

Create a Communal Art Installation with Found Objects: You can approach this exercise in two ways, depending on the setting. If you are in a location that has natural abundance, such as rocks, leaves, feathers, etc, ask participants to explore and find an item to which they feel a connection. Alternatively, you can supply everyday household objects for the group to select from. The goal is to create a living installation together: participants take turns adding an item to the collective piece. Once completed, invite the group to observe the finished piece and see what it reveals about collaborative creativity.

Practice Mindful Seeing: This is an exercise of what our friend Kerry calls "exquisite noticing." In a group setting, invite participants to take a slow, mindful walk (5-10 minutes) around the space (whether indoors or outdoors), paying close attention to the visual field, including colors, shapes, textures, patterns, light and shadow, and so on. Ask each person to take one photo of what they found the most vivid or compelling. This is not about taking beautiful pictures, but about really seeing the world with fresh eyes. Then ask each person to share what they saw, including the photo they took. In our creative gatherings, this exercise has sparked some very insightful discussions about the nature of art itself. It can also be a great, low-stakes way for people to begin exploring their creativity in a safe context.

Lead a Word Throw: Decide on a writing prompt such as "What I need for my creativity is . . . ." Let participants know they will have 10 or 15 minutes to do this exercise. Also, let them know that every 45-60 seconds, you will read out a word for them to incorporate into their writing. Choose these words randomly from any text. After the allotted time period, ask participants to discuss their writing process. People are often surprised at their ability to weave in these random words and delighted to hear how others met the challenge. This exercise helps build trust in the spontaneity of the creative process as well as the ability to meet hurdles when they arise.

CHAPTER TWELVE

SYNCREATE YOUR LIFE

Congratulations! You have completed your tour through the creative process from start to finish. Now, it's time to practice the strategies of Play, Plan, and Produce. Take a moment to imagine yourself using the Syncreate process to successfully complete and celebrate your creative work. Imagine you are being recognized for reaching your goal: What does that look like and feel like? Who is there with you, cheering you on? Who would you most like to thank? What does this project inspire for you and for others? How could you continue to build upon what you have created? Trust that the world is a better place for the creative contributions you are making.

OVERVIEW OF THE CREATIVE PROCESS

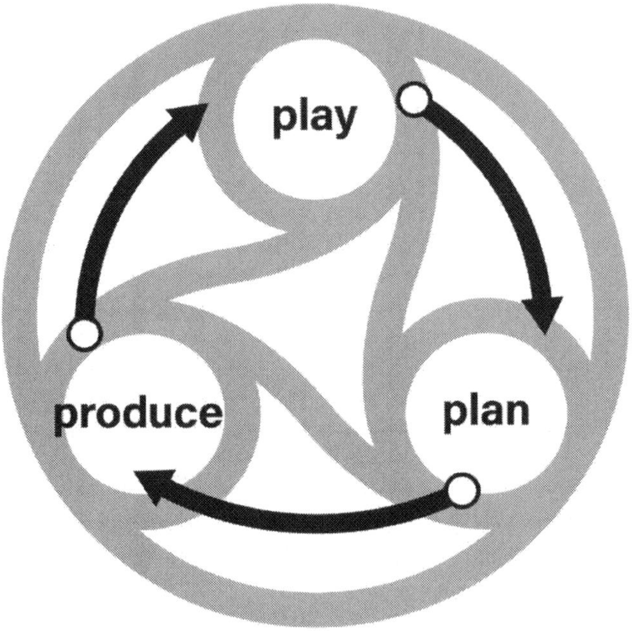

Returning to the Syncreate model image, we have now come full circle in the journey of creation. We've organized this often messy and chaotic process into three major phases, Play, Plan, and Produce. Chapters 1-3 described the playful elements of creative ideation, skill building, and experimentation. Chapters 4-6 explored the more linear components of designing the map and formalizing the plan, as well as how to navigate the inevitable challenge of getting lost and finding your way. Chapters 7-9 focused on production, including iteration, feedback, and fruition. Chapters 10 and 11 discussed how teams, organizations, and communities can use this approach for creative collaboration.

We believe that by employing the tools of Play, Plan, and Produce, you will unlock key insights about your own creativity. If you regularly make your creativity a priority, you will improve and even gain a sense of mastery regarding your craft. There may be setbacks and disappointments along the way, of course. How many of us wish our abilities matched our aspirations? To close this gap, we must commit to the practice of honing our skills over time and building an artistic community.

Even though we might well end up somewhere completely different than we imagined, we do find ourselves in a larger, more expanded world, with new ideas, insights, and companions along the path. Some of the most important creative and scientific insights happened not because of dumb luck, but because their discoverers had been diligently working on their craft, day after day and year after year, when they "suddenly" stumbled upon something new and innovative. In other words, creativity and discipline are interconnected. In order to build confidence in our ability to produce, we must return, again and again, to the stages of playing and planning; it's a recursive process. Additionally, if we can learn to identify our best practices, we can both decrease our creative suffering and increase our creative joy.

Art is vital, as it provides a forum for learning our most profound lessons. It has the potential to affirm our deepest selves, facilitate connections, and strengthen communities. The world can seem a cold and indifferent place, especially when it comes to our art. But being open to the process and the people we meet in our journey can offer as much delight as the moments of creative fruition. Indeed, the more we connect and deepen our relationship to the process through incremental goals and accountability partnerships, the more we say yes to our work and to the work of others.

Can you create? Absolutely. And cocreate too. Let us all discover the power of collaboration. Syncreate can open new doors. You learn a powerful process—and in only three steps, but don't be deceived. These begin with play (which is crucial), followed by planning and producing. Each has its own components. The plan is based on knowledge of creative process, and you will find the satisfaction and even joy that can follow. Problems are natural along the way, but let us accept and maneuver these, and guess what? They too are part of the path! In our holistic, dynamic, nonlinear, and deeply interconnected world, cocreation is an ever more vital and engaging priority.

—Ruth Richards, M.D. Ph.D.
Author & Creativity Scholar

So, in other words, *you got this.* Accept the reality that the creative process involves a fundamental reconsideration of our ideas and ways of knowing. Learn to find satisfaction in the small moments of accomplishment. Find a system for setting micro goals. By doing these things, you will find your waypoints and you will find yourself.

In Chapter 8, we encouraged you to consider giving back to other artists, and here, in closing, we want to offer this idea: When you think about giving up, contemplate the good work you will do as a mentor and friend, peer and advocate, accountability partner and faith tender. Think of the other creatives you could support down the road once you've reached your goal. The world needs you to stay on the path of creating your art. So, do it. Allow joy to be your companion, and extend it to others.

BIBLIOGRAPHY AND RECOMMENDED RESOURCES

Amabile, T. M. (1996). *Creativity in context*. Boulder, CO: Westview Press.

Amabile, T. M. (1998). A model for creativity and innovation in organizations. *Research in Organizational Behavior, 10*, 123-167.

Barrington, J. (2002). *Writing the memoir: From truth to art,* (2nd edition). Portland, OR: The Eighth Mountain Press.

Barth, J. (1987). *The tidewater tales*. New York, NY: G.P. Putnam and Sons.

Blake, A. (2018). *Your body is your brain: Leverage your somatic intelligence to find purpose, build resilience, deepen relationships and lead more powerfully.* Truckee. CA: Trokay Press.

Bolte-Taylor, J. (2008). *My stroke of insight: A brain scientist's personal journey.* New York, NY: Viking Adult.

Bolte-Taylor, J. (2008). My stroke of insight (Ted Talk). https://www.ted.com/talks/jill_bolte_taylor_my_stroke_of_insight?language=en

Brown, B. (2018). *Dare to lead.* New York, NY: Random House.

Daido Loori, J. (2005). *The Zen of creativity: Cultivating your artistic life.* New York, NY: Ballantine Books.

Cameron, J. (1992). *The artist's way: A spiritual path to higher creativity.* New York, NY: TarcherPerigree.

Campbell, J. with Moyers, B. (1988). *The power of myth.* (B. S. Flowers, Ed.). New York, NY: Anchor Books.

Dickens, C. (1860/1998). *Great expectations.* Oxford, UK: Oxford University Press.

Duhigg, C. (2016, Feb. 25). What Google learned from its quest to build a perfect team. *The New York Times Magazine.* www.nytimes.com/2016/02/28/magazine/what-google-learned-from-its-quest-to-build-the-perfect-team.html

Dweck, C. (2006). *Mindset: The new psychology of success.* New York, NY: Ballantine Books.

Gladwell, M. (2008). *Outliers: The story of success.* New York, NY: Little, Brown & Co.

Glass, I. (2013). Ira Glass on storytelling. https://www.youtube.com/watch?v=f6ezU57J8YI

Goslin-Jones, T. (2011). Using expressive arts to transform the workplace. In N. Rogers (Ed.), *The creative connection for groups: Person-Centered Expressive Arts for healing and social change* (pp. 354-357). Palo Alto, CA: Science and Behavior Books.

Ideo. (2021). Design thinking defined. *Ideo Design Thinking*. https://designthinking.ideo.com

Klemperer, P. (2016, June). 'Woodshedding': A leadership practice worth considering. *Jazz Thinking: The Jazz Ezine*. http://www.jazzthink.com/ezine/1606_ezine.html

Lawton, B. & Rosenfeld, J. (2008). *Write free: Attracting the creative life*. Glen Ellen: CA: Kulupi Press.

May, R. (1975). *The courage to create*. New York, NY: W. W. Norton & Co.

Mind Tools. (2021). SMART goals: How to make your goals achievable. https://www.mindtools.com/pages/article/smart-goals.htm

Miyashiro, M. R. (2011). *The empathy factor: Your competitive advantage for personal, team, and business success*. Encinitas, CA: Puddle Jumper Press.

Mitchell, S. (Ed.). (1988). *Tao te ching*. New York, NY: Harper Perennial.

Nielsen. D. (2017). *The divergent and convergent thinking book: How to enhance your innovative thinking, an exercise book.* (Csm Stk edition). London, England: Laurence King Publishing.

Oppong, T. (2017, Nov. 30). For a more creative brain, embrace constraints. Inc. https://www.inc.com/thomas-oppong/for-a-more-creative-brain-embrace-constraints.html

Padow, J. (2017). Using fiction within nonfiction to navigate difficult emotional terrain. https://brevitymag.com/craft-essays/using-fiction-within-nonfiction-to-navigate-difficult-emotional-terrain/

Richards, R. (Ed.). (2007). *Everyday creativity and new views of human nature: Psychological, social, and spiritual perspectives.* Washington, DC: American Psychological Association.

Richards, R. (2018). *Everyday creativity and the healthy mind: Dynamic new paths for self and society.* London, UK: Palgrave Macmillan.

Ries, E. (2011). *Lean startup: How today's entrepreneurs use continuous innovation to create radically successful businesses.* New York, NY: Crown Business.

Romanyshyn, R. (2013). *The wounded researcher: Research with soul in mind.* New Orleans, LA: Spring Journal Books.

Rothouse, M. (2020), *A mindful approach to team creativity and collaboration in organizations: Creating a culture of innovation.* London, UK: Palgrave Macmillan.

Rozovsky, J. (2015, Nov. 17). The five keys to a successful Google team. https://rework.withgoogle.com/blog/five-keys-to-a-successful-google-team/

Runco, M. A. (1991). *Divergent thinking.* Norwood, NJ. Ablex Publishing Corporation.

Runco, M. (Ed.) (1994). *Problem finding, problem solving, and creativity.* Norwood, NJ: Ablex.

Runco, M. A. & Pritzker, S. R. (2020). *Encyclopedia of creativity* (3rd Ed.). Amsterdam: Academic Press/Elsevier.

Schierse Leonard, L. (2000). *The call to create: Celebrating acts of imagination.* New York, NY: Harmony.

Siegel, D. (2017). *Mind: A journey to the heart of being human.* New York, NY: W. W. Norton & Co.

Suzuki, S. (1970/2007). *Zen mind, beginner's mind.* Boston, MA: Weatherhill.

Wallas, G. (1926/2014). *The art of thought.* Tunbridge Wells, UK. Solis Press.

ABOUT THE AUTHORS

Charlotte Gullick grew up in a very rural town in Northern California, among the redwoods and the heavy rains of Mendocino County. She is the first in her family to graduate from college, and she holds a BA in English/Literature, a MA in English/Creative Writing from UC Davis, and a MFA in Creative Nonfiction from the Institute of American Indian Arts. Charlotte writes fiction, memoir, and nonfiction and is Chair of the Creative Writing Department at Austin Community College. She teaches regularly for the Writers' League of Texas and also works with individuals on specific writing projects. Her work has been published in *Brevity, The Rumpus, The Best of Brevity*, and *Dogwood: A Journal of Poetry and Prose*, among others. She has won the Evergreen State College Teaching Excellence Award, a NISOD Teaching Award, the Gold Star for Teaching and Mentorship from American Short Fiction, a Colorado Council on the Arts Poetry Fellowship, a Christopher Isherwood Fiction Fellowship, and writing residencies from MacDowell, Ragdale, and San Ysidro.

Melinda Rothouse is a creativity, career, and leadership development coach and consultant, as well as an educator, facilitator, and public speaker. She is also a singer, songwriter, and bass player with many years of training and experience as a performing musician. Her other creative pursuits include contemplative photography and writing. She holds a BA in biopsychology, master's degrees in religious studies and performance studies, and a Ph.D. in psychology with a specialization in creativity studies. She is a longtime meditator and mindfulness practitioner teacher, and leads workshops and retreats in contemplative arts and creativity. She is the author of *A Mindful Approach to Team Creativity and Collaboration in Organizations: Creating a Culture of Innovation*, published by Palgrave Macmillan in 2020.

Dreux Carpenter holds a B.A. in Art, and an M.A. and M.F.A. in Writing and Consciousness. He has over 25 years of experience as a Graphic Designer/Art Director. He served as Vice President of the Writers' League of Texas from 2019 to 2021.

Made in the USA
Columbia, SC
04 November 2021

48374370R00089